The Magic Land

Designing Your Own Enchanted Garden

The Magic Land

Designing Your Own Enchanted Garden

by

Julie Moir Messervy
Illustrations by Barbara M. Berger

MACMILLAN • USA

MACMILLAN
A Simon & Schuster Macmillan Company
1633 Broadway
New York, NY 10019-6785

Macmillan Publishing books may be purchased for business or sales promotional
use. For information please write: Special Markets Department, Macmillan
Publishing USA, 1633 Broadway, New York, NY 10019.

Library of Congress Cataloging-in-Publication Data
Messervy, Julie Moir.
    The magic land : designing your own enchanted garden / Julie Moir
Messervy ; illustrations by Barbara Berger.
        p.   cm.
    ISBN: 0-02-862091-7
    1. Gardens—Design.   2. Gardens—Philosophy.   3. Gardens—Pictorial
works.   I. Title.
    SB473.M446   1998
    712'.6—dc21   97-31531
                                                             CIP

Manufactured in the United States of America
10 9 8 7 6 5 4 3 2 1

Book and cover design by Scott Meola

To Paul and Helen Messervy

Contents

Part Two
Making Gardens

Acknowledgments

This little book has been a pleasure to produce, thanks to the imagination and industry of my editor, Laurie Barnett, and the creative vision of my illustrator Barbara Berger, who also helped with the final editing and organization of the book. Thanks also to Scott Meola for his magical design and Francesca Drago, Sharon Lee, and Rebecca Payes for production.

Special thanks go to my agent, Lew Grimes, for his steadfast support and enthusiasm for my ideas, and to my wise and patient assistant, Edie Murphy.

My life was graced by Theo Colburn's clarity of vision, Callie West's understanding and experience, and the *I Ching*'s unerring counsel.

To my family, I offer this book as one small token of my love.

PART ONE

Dreaming Gardens

Once upon a time, when we were very young, we each possessed a place of enchantment and dreams. To reach it, we would don seven-league boots and travel over days and weeks and through many kingdoms. Sometimes this land was reached through magical portals—a secret door at the back of a wardrobe or a rainbow that we could cross to a valley far away. Sometimes we found it in books—in fairy tales or adventure stories; as wonderlands or books of marvels. Usually, it was right in our own backyards, where our imaginations could run free in a safe haven close to home. Some of these places were light-filled; others were dark. A stick fort became a crystal palace; a boulder an unreachable mountain; a basement a moist and scary cavern far beneath the earth. The clouds sheltered unicorns, tree roots harbored elves, and monsters dwelled under our beds, ready to pounce the moment our eyes finally closed. Flowers became gardens, a birdbath the sea. In these enchanted landscapes, from our enchanted home, we grew to great maturity, but never grew old.

Chapter 1

The Magic Land

*Your garden is a
magic land in your life.*

'VE come to look at your property to help you design a garden. I walk in, shake your hand, and look around, enjoying your house and its contents while getting a sense of you through what you have already created in your home. We sit at your kitchen table and talk about what you want. You explain that you've lived in this house awhile and have made it your own but you're completely unsure about what to do with the outside. You don't know how to begin. We stroll around your site while I continue to hear your story and ask questions.

What should your garden look like? I see it as a place distilled from the elements of your imagination, your memories, and your dreams. It is my job to help you realize and grow this garden; to help you give birth to it and to give it form. But first you must supply the seeds that will provide its character and its structure, and you must nourish it and love it into being.

You tell me you want something beautiful. Easy to care for. Special. Personal. You want a place that feels serene and is one that you can sink your hands into, getting away from phones, faxes, cars, kids, and responsibilities. And you don't know what it looks like — not yet.

I will try to create a garden that is yours, feels right, looks good all year round, and serves as a sanctuary for your soul. But even more than these good qualities, it must have this essential ingredient: It must feel like a "magic land" — something out of your imagination that has somehow sprung to life in your own backyard.

Because I can't work with everyone who wants a garden, I decided to write this book instead. This is a little idea book for your imagination: full of concepts, images, and principles that can help you take what is now a "yard" and make it into a "garden" — a land full of meaning and magic.

EXERCISE: START A DREAM GARDEN JOURNAL

When I say the words *magic land*, what places do you think of? What elements make up your magic land? What feelings are evoked? Write down or draw up the features that come to mind in a journal that you keep at your side as you dream about your garden. Continue adding ideas as you read this book.

When I answer this question, a collage of images appears in my mind: the woods behind our first house, the skating pond, the scary attic, and the billowing clouds that would form fairy castles across the sky. A grape arbor, snapdragons, roses, and peonies. A little lakeside cottage nestled in the pines, a cupola atop a Victorian home, and a faraway path through a jungle lit only by the moon. My memories spill over with images of gardens: Marrakeshi, Mughal, Zen, cottage, classical, romantic, lush, and spare, stone on stone. So many others, but the very last image is my own land today: slowly becoming as magical as the places I have known.

I am sure that you have a different set of images in mind. Your magic land may come from parks you've played in as a child, children's books your parents read to you, paintings you've studied, trips you've taken, streams you've fished in. Wherever you've lived, whatever your background, you hold images of magic lands in your mind.

The enchanted realms of childhood were places where the everyday world disappeared and time stood still; they were dream kingdoms, created and nurtured by you.

Think back to all those little nooks that you created in your youth. What of the hiding places under the rhododendron bush or beneath the kitchen table; the tree houses erected in nearby scrub or woods; the dollhouses created in closets and clubhouses under the eaves; the dams built in streams and castles mounted atop boulders in the park? Remember daydreaming while nestled deep within blankets on a crisp winter morning or becoming engrossed in an adventure tale while curled up in an easy chair in front of a fire. At those moments, your world felt transformed; you felt as though you were inhabiting an enchanted land.

The Magic Land

• • • • • •

Your garden must feel like a "magic land" . . .

The Magic Land

• • • • • •

. . . something out of your imagination that has somehow sprung to life in your own backyard.

The Magic Land

• • • • • •

Nothing has changed except that you have grown up. And you still find magic lands in your life. You go hiking, fishing, or scuba diving. You read books of literature, of history, of fantasy, or you attend concerts, exhibitions, go to church. You take long walks through the park with your dog. You sing, dance, paint, or play an instrument. You travel to tropical islands or to mountain resorts; to cities of high culture or remote villages. At home, you set things off as special; you bring order to a messy room. You decorate your house at holiday time. You make love. You daydream. You create. You garden.

I don't believe that individuals can really live without a magic land in their lives; for me it is a place where the intersection of dreams, creativity, and joy are given three-dimensional form either in one's mind or on one's land. Without it, we would all become flattened by the rituals and responsibilities of life; hardened to our lot rather than softened by its possibilities. The act of creating a magic land in our busy lives is not a luxury but a necessity, because it fills us with good feelings and brings us a sense of wholeness.

A magic land does not come with a particular size or configuration. It may be as intimate as a terrarium or as immense as a rain forest, as tiny as a bonsai or as huge as a redwood tree. What makes a garden into a magic land is your own particular vision of it. It is a place that resonates with meaning for you, that allows you to feel at home, that brings you back to your true self; a place that, when you no longer occupy it, you have still left a little bit of yourself behind.

Magic lands are places to which you can withdraw. But when you have created enough magic lands in your life, you can learn to share them with others, either with a child, a lover, a neighbor, or with a group of like-minded friends or family. Others change a magic land into a place of wonderful richness and joy. A goal is to have both places of community and places of retreat.

For so many of us, this unconscious need to create a magic land in our lives happens most directly and literally when we garden. Working with the materials of the earth—plants, stones, dirt—and manipulating them so they are transformed into a space of beauty and meaning is the very artistry of garden design. The evanescence of flowers and their natural birth-death-rebirth cycle coexists with the permanence of stones; the silvery magic of a still pool contrasts with the musky palpability of compost, mulch, and dirt—the growing medium that together with water allows a garden to live.

The problem is not how to grow those plants but what should they be? And how and where to place them? What is the larger form in which they sit?

When I make a garden for someone, I could set out stones, trees, paths, fences, and plantings in such a way that they fulfill my ideal of what a good garden should look like. Yet it is my responsibility to understand the components of my clients' magic land and to create the garden accordingly. The result of my endeavors should not only match their ideals, but also go beyond them—we each should come away with a new kind of magic land that we have created together and that no one has ever seen nor ventured into before. Then we have been successful.

SEE THE WORLD AS A GARDEN

One overriding principle dominates this book: See the world as a garden. Everywhere you look, whether in the inner city or far out in the country; whether you live in an apartment building or own a grand estate, there is beauty to behold if only you know how to notice it. One of the delights of design is that ideas are everywhere: If you are creating a little stream in your backyard, you can learn about how water works by studying a natural riverscape, a drainage ditch, or even a series of puddles after a rainstorm. If you want to create a leafy corner in your apartment, then you can walk to a nearby forest to learn about canopy, understory, and forest floor and reinterpret those ideas with potted plants. I find ideas for my designs everywhere I look—in the whorl of a tree trunk, a logo for a restaurant, the jut of a stone along a favorite walk, or the glint of light through a neighbor's grove of trees. I see four cardinals chase one another throughout the neighborhood, and I feel wonderful. No matter how saddened I become by the events of life, when I see the world as a garden, I feel better.

And when you start to actually create a garden, whether on your land, in your home, for a public place, or through your imagination, your joy in the world around you radiates outward into the lives of others.

Chapter 2
Mother Earth: Magic Vantages upon the World

Magic derives from seven archetypal vantage points.

NE of my favorite clients is a recently widowed woman who lives with her dogs in a nearby city. She had a back fenced-in corner that hadn't been maintained for years, and she decided to make a garden there. After finding out her general needs, I drew up some schematic sketches and then made a mock-up on the ground for her to walk through. I brought in samples of leaves and boughs from trees and shrubs I thought she might appreciate and soon formed a planting palette that seemed to suit her particular taste. We built the garden slowly, laying out the low circular sitting walls, then moving to the sinuous brick paths, then to the large trees, smaller trees and shrubs, and finally to the perennials and ground covers. She had strong design and placement ideas about each layer that we built, improving the garden with every decision that she made. In the end, we created a garden that could only be my client's, because her hand and fine eye was present every step of the way.

Most important to me was to engage her spirit. As we worked together, I learned that my client was a practicing Buddhist and wanted to create a refuge for "creatures," especially in the winter months. We chose trees that would offer protected perches and nesting places for the flocks of birds that made their home in her garden. We chose berrying shrubs as an additional winter food source along with the seed she regularly put out for squirrels, chipmunks, and birds. We hollowed out a stone and filled it with water as a source of liquid for the wildlife, complete with inlet, outlet, and heating unit. Now, all winter long, the animals line up to get a drink! Within this little wildlife sanctuary in the city, we also created sitting places where my client could view the activities of her creatures close-up, as well as a little memorial garden over the cremated remains of three of her beloved dogs.

This garden is a tiny portion of a bigger garden called Mother Earth, a sanctuary that protects and sustains life, possesses inherent beauty, provides a place for the imagination and a resting place for the spirit. By giving birth to her garden, my client has given life to not only flora but also fauna; by nurturing her creatures, she sustains the earth and her soul.

EXERCISE: CHILDHOOD DAYDREAMING PLACES

Close your eyes and think back to your childhood. Where did you go to daydream? What places did you find for reverie, for reflection? Write or draw your reactions to this question in your design notebook. You'll draw on it for inspiration as you read.

Perhaps you climbed high up into a maple tree or rode swiftly across fields bareback on a pony or spent hours lying facedown on the grass, watching the insects at work in the soil. You may have found places of refuge inside the house: practicing the piano, gazing out at the world from an attic window, or reading by flashlight under the sheets when you were supposed to be asleep. Or you sought out institutions in the city—its arboreta, museums, libraries, or coffeehouses. Perhaps there were faraway places you visited: a cherished grandparent's garden, a sleep-away camp in a remote wilderness, or a family car trip to a magnificent national park.

List your childhood memories of special places, and you'll be surprised by the feelings that this exercise evokes. Recently, two students cried as they sought to explain their daydreaming drawings to the audience at a seminar I was teaching. One woman sobbed, filled with sadness that her own children could not explore her neighborhood as freely as she had as a child, due to increased crime. Another woman was overcome with emotion as she explained that her daydreaming place, built on for new development, was now gone. My response was that whether they still exist or not, we carry these places in our hearts forever.

The Magic Land

• • • • • •

As I have written in previous books, we each explore Mother Earth as we explored the landscape of our mother, finding places of comfort, security, and protection in her crevices and folds, and vantages for viewing from her cliffs and hills. Just as baby birds are hatched and fed from the nest, eventually flying off to make their own lives; so too are we born, held close, nurtured, and then offered independence to become landscapes on our own. We explore our Mother Earth as "the creatures" explore my client's garden; we feel comfortable in our world by finding our place within it.

The world becomes a magic land when filled with a mix of places of comfort and security, exhilaration and independence. Some years ago, when I became a mother, I realized that my body formed a landscape for my children, in fact, the very first landscape that they had ever experienced. As embryos, they were immersed in the fluid of my womb. As newborns, they were thrust into the world and immediately swaddled and wrapped tightly, seeing the world from a series of cavelike spaces—cradles, cribs, and snuglis, always bundled and blanketed. As soon as they were able to hold up their heads, they started to look at the world from my lap, held in by my harbor-like embrace, but able to look out from a position of security. As toddlers, they chose to get off my lap and creep, toddle, and finally walk out to the edge of their viewable world, always checking back with me, but enjoying a promontory-like freedom that they hadn't known before. This phase lasted for many years, until adolescence approached, when the children made gestures to become separate and detached from me as parent, and chose instead to become islands—little landscapes of their own adrift on the sea of life.

All this time I have been a landscape to them, I also have been climbing the mountain of maturity, trying to find the freedom to reach the summit where I need to learn to be alone and free. I expect that all of us will reach the last vantage point of our lives— our deaths—when we ascend to the sky: the place of transcendence, enlightenment, wisdom, and the realm of the spirit—the place where we leave the landscape as we've known it behind.

I believe that these seven vantage points: the sea, the cave, the harbor, the promontory, the island, the mountain, and the sky, are archetypal places—the original patterns on which we model all other places that we experience. They are the first magic places of our lives, and as such, create strong feelings in us. When we come to a place that reminds us of one of these archetypal vantage points, we often reexperience the early emotions associated with it.

But such vantages may not necessarily always conjure up pleasant memories. Early traumatic experiences can render certain places horrific, rather than joyful. Some years ago, I became phobic toward elevators, tunnels, bridges, highways, and airplanes and found it difficult to maneuver normally in the world. At first, I avoided contact with these spaces but inevitably found that I had to start to deal with my fears in order to go out to work. I developed coping mechanisms to combat the panic that would arise when I entered a tunnel or an elevator or when I took off in an airplane, and little by little I was able to regain my trust in the world.

In my experience, the phobias that I had for places that I associated with a loss of control meant that places of security and comfort became even more important than they had before. I imagine that the same is true for others as well. No one can survive without a safe place to call one's own even if it is only a space in one's mind. I describe the following seven archetypes of space as joyful places—as magic lands—but I know that the opposite can also be true, depending on one's own experiences.

The archetypes represent the life cycle from birth until death that we each go through—a spiral that leads from sea through different landscapes to sky and then back again, perhaps at a deeper or a higher level of awareness each time we cycle through. The archetypes represent places of meaning and magic that you occupy, consciously or unconsciously, in which you move, physically, psychologically, emotionally, and spiritually, toward wholeness.

THE SEA: IMMERSION

Each of us loves the feeling of being immersed in a place that offers safety, comfort, protection, and love—a place that feels blanketed in softness. This feeling is probably a memory trace that comes from being an embryo immersed in the intrauterine sea of our mother's womb.

As we grow older, this sealike experience of space is something that we continually seek to recreate. When we swim underwater, snorkel, or scuba dive, we relive our embryonic existence directly. When we bathe, shower, or enter spas, steam baths, or saunas, we feel soothed just as we did in the serenity of the womb. Even potentially fearful immersion experiences through the forces of nature can be exhilarating under the right circumstances: being caught in a thick fog bank, a heavy rainstorm, a blinding snowstorm or sandstorm. Architecture, too, can engulf you in an inspirational way: Entering a cathedral, you feel a sense of reverence and awe as a tiny being immersed in a huge space of filtered light, music, incense, and spiritual symbolism.

We feel the same way in an ancient grove of towering trees, be they pines, redwoods, or bamboo. At Tolstoy's ancestral home, Yasnaya Polyana, one feels delightfully submerged within the leafy canopy that flourishes over his beloved landscape. His garden is made up of groves of tall trees: beech *allées*, birch plantations, apple orchards, and fir forests that emerge from blankets of Russian wildflowers that seem to love the muted light.

Our ability to become immersed within a space happens not only on the physical level, but also on mental and psychological levels.

Architecture, too, can engulf you in an inspirational way: Entering a cathedral, you feel a sense of reverence and awe.

When we hear a symphonic concert or don earphones in a subway, we surround ourselves with music; when we read an engrossing book, whether a novel, a work of history, or a poem, we become transported to another place and time set by the words and images of the author; when we concentrate, meditate, daydream, or sleep, we become mentally immersed in those activities. This is the kind of experience we seek to create in our gardens: to envelop our senses in the sights, sounds, scents, and feelings of a beautiful planted place. Our first immersion experience—what I call the sea—becomes a touchstone for all immersion experiences and is the very first magic land of our lives.

THE CAVE: NESTLING

Think back to a little place you loved, intimate and tucked away. Perhaps it had a narrow view onto the bigger world. It might have been a little hideaway, a cubbyhole, a spot under the grand piano, or a place beneath the basement stairs; it might have been a secret niche under the porch or beneath the forsythia bush outside in your backyard. All these niches were nestling places that you could get inside of and find a space for dreaming.

The need for little places probably comes from being swaddled in your parents' arms. This nestling feeling was fulfilled by the architecture of babyhood: cradles, cribs, snuglis, bassinets—all small places that almost perfectly fit the form (and feeling) of the newborn who has emerged from the serenity and safety of its mother's womb. This sensibility is something that we seek again and again in our world. We answer the need by inhabiting tree houses, bowers, summerhouses; nooks, alcoves, retreats, eaves. We find little houses: igloos, wigwams, teepees, cottages, pavilions, dovecotes, snuggeries. We love to look out through portholes, leaded glass, screens; we seek out bays, bow windows, rose windows, lattice, skylights, and transoms. The small size of the interior space and the aperture of its opening are what make a space feel like a cave.

In the natural world, caves abound. Burrows, lairs, dens, tunnels, and nests are all cavelike enclosures. In a garden, we require hutlike nestling places to feel secure as we daydream. The trellis, pergola, porch, gazebo, arbor, or bench each offers us a shelter that combines mental refreshment with physical rest.

THE HARBOR: EMBRACE

A harbor is a haven, a space of enclosure; an area of refuge for body and soul. As an inlet off the open sea, a harbor, port, gulf, cove, or bay offers the protection of calm waters, the enfolding embrace of the surrounding arms of land, and a secure anchorage for mooring. A garden can be described as a harbor because it is a safe haven and a sacred realm that lies distinct from other land around it. Without enclosure, is it possible to create a magic land at all?

A harbor is an important image for garden designers the world over, for all great gardens feel set apart from the outside world. At Sissinghurst Castle Garden, the home of Vita Sackville-West and Harold Nicolson, the open expanse of chartreuse mustard weed fields that paints the Kentish landscape in spring is suddenly interrupted by Sissinghurst's moat and the strong architectural framework of its gardens. Organized as enclosures within enclosures, each garden harbors intimately scaled but richly varied plantings, laid out along axial paths but allowed to spill informally. Oriental gardens, too, are always enclosed. One of the most celebrated gardens in Suzhou, Shi Zi Lin, is enclosed by a high whitewashed wall punctuated by an elegant plum-shaped door and pomegranate-shaped windows. The teeming city is thus relegated to the outside, and only welcome visitors are invited within.

The Magic Land
• • • • • •

A harbor feels like a sanctuary created by something that encircles.

A semicircular bench looks and feels like a literal harbor, a space set just off the main path for viewing a focal point, such as a nearby piece of sculpture or a distant view. A park bench can also feel harborlike, especially when set with its back against a thick tree trunk, shrub border, hill, or building. Different from a cave or little hut that fits one's body, a harbor feels like a sanctuary created by something that encircles: a ring or belt of trees, a square surrounded by town houses, a cloister, a hedged garden room. A magic land derives its enchanted quality by its distinction from the everyday world; a garden requires enclosure to feel magic.

THE PROMONTORY: EXTENSION

A promontory is like a pier that extends far into the sea; a peninsula, a precipice, a frontier; being at the very edge of the world. When you first wriggled off your parent's lap and started crawling, then standing unsteadily and toddling across a vast expanse to explore the unknown, you became a promontory. You found yourself enticed by places that were far-flung or forbidden: You climbed the stairs, wandered too far in the park, or escaped out the front gate to watch the cars whiz by. As you grew, you sought adventure by climbing trees and play structures, exploring nearby forests, damming up brooks and streams, and going into town by yourself or with friends. From toddlerhood to adolescence, you made forays into the world, while always returning to the relative security of home and parents.

This phase is symbolized by transitional elements: thresholds that bridge the space between one place and another. At its extreme, a promontory stands somewhere between land, water, and sky—it is the thinnest spit of earth pushed as far as possible into the sea and covered over by the sky.

As you grew, you sought adventure by climbing trees.

Anything that is an appendage to a structure that juts into the landscape is a promontory. Therefore, a parapet—the turned-up railing that keeps one from falling over a precipitous edge—is a promontory. In your garden, it is a balustrade, a balcony, a porch, or a deck. A terrace is a promontory: It acts like the tongue of the house that protrudes into the landscape, allowing you to feel as if you are sitting in the house and in the garden at the same time. Promontories allow us the exhilaration of getting to the very edge of our known world.

THE ISLAND: SEPARATENESS

The island is a promontory that is cut off from the land. It is a little landscape that floats on the sea, surrounded on all sides by water; independent, detached, secure as a world unto itself. It represents the moment in life when you choose the freedom of separateness; you become an adolescent.

My fifteen-year-old son is an island. His six-foot-two frame holds a body that is quite distinct from his parents; his mind is beginning to follow. He voices his opinions, chooses his own style, ventures into new terrain, and requires more privacy than when he was a promontory, still psychologically attached to his family. From adolescence on, we seek to be with others to erase our loneliness: We fall in love, we seek out trusting friends and comrades, we associate and collaborate in our work, we marry, we procreate. But in the end, we remain detached islands, floating on the sea of life.

In Oriental gardens, islands have traditionally been used to represent longevity and prosperity. The Japanese often create "tortoise" and "crane" islands in their landscapes: rocky islets with stones placed to resemble a great sea turtle with its head, flippers, shell, and tail; or a crane with its graceful body, neck, and wings. They believe that "the tortoise lives a thousand years, the crane ten thousand years," and this good fortune will follow the owner of such a garden.

We create little island havens away from the workaday world in places that feel cut off and remote: in forests, on mountaintops, and on islands themselves. We travel to paradise isles in the sun; and we lie on blankets looking up into the heavens, imagining life on the islands in the sky: the stars, the moon, the galaxies of the universe. We become islands while occupying a chaise longue, floating in a swimming pool, or fantasizing about a magic carpet ride—whenever we inhabit a faraway space either physically or mentally. Becoming an island from time to time is a magic trick that we all can conjure up and that is necessary to our survival as individuals and as imaginative souls.

THE MOUNTAIN: TRANSFORMATION

I think that I am in the mountain stage of my life now. A mountain is akin to an island, but raised high off the ground, a pinnacle on which we can stand above the world and from which we gain perspective. Climbing the mountain is an eventful journey, sometimes torturous as one ekes one's way up and up and up, clinging to the smallest of footholds, afraid to look down. But it can also be blissful, as we encounter broad alpine meadows and upland streams, where we stand secure, high up at the edge of the earth. Climbing a mountain requires steadfastness, fortitude, and guts to get to the top, and it requires vision—the vision to look upon where you have been and to see it as part of a continuous whole. I haven't reached the top of my mountain yet. In the meantime, I will continue to make garden mounts along the way.

The mountain in our gardens is a mount, a little high place with a 360-degree view that you long to occupy. A tree house is a mount with a cave on top; a cupola is a mount with an enclosure around it; the famed gardens at Williamsburg's Governor's Palace have a lofty mount from which you can view the intricate hedged maze below.

Another type of garden mount is one that you climb in your imagination instead of with your feet. Any kind of vertical focal point—a birdhouse, a special tree, a distant view of a mountain or a building, a statue—can be an imaginative mount in the landscape. Orienting your garden around a vertical "mount" can galvanize your design—think of how strongly a vertical accent affects the landscape around it: A lighthouse or tower draws all eyes to it; a single topiary tree becomes the centerpiece for a garden room. A garden mount is a symbolic peak that acts as both archetypal vantage point and focal object.

THE SKY: TRANSCENDENCE

In the sky we are finally able to transcend the landscape. Think of the ways we physically seek the sky: We swing high into the air, climb to the tallest branch, jump on trampolines, and ride on Ferris wheels. The more daring of us bungee jump or parachute jump or float through the air in a glider; some even become astronauts. Flying in airplanes allows us to inhabit the sky, where we ride inside a cave way above the clouds, enjoying an aerial perspective of Mother Earth.

Yet while it is a rare occasion that we actually inhabit the sky, it is more common for us to *feel* as if we do when we are in a transcendent state of mind. A skylike euphoria is reflected in the "highs" of our life: the wonderment of falling in love, bearing a child, being intensely creative or physical, having an orgasm, or altering our consciousness through meditation or chemicals. Each of these states takes us out of our normal pace of existence, where our thoughts and emotions are so full and so purely focused that our mind nearly transcends our body. Anyone who has experienced a mind-body separation or out-of-body experience knows how terrifying such a state can be—one never knows when and if the two will recombine again as one. However, accounts of near-death experiences suggest that the ultimate moment of transcending the body to become pure spirit is not fearful, but joyful—finally ascending to the light of the sky and the heavens above.

Our emotions are quietly but constantly mirrored by the moods of the magic land above, the sky. We feel hope as dawn breaks in bands of peach and purple; anxiety as lightning screeches across a stormy sky; sadness as gray clouds screen out all trace of the sun; contentment as we bask in the weak rays of an Indian summer day; soulfulness as the orb dips softly beneath the sea and switches places with the moon rising silently in the blackness of the nighttime sky.

How can we bring the feeling of sky into our gardens? It needs to be captured, somehow, and set into a frame. We can direct attention to it by erecting sculptures that point upward. We can paint the sky on our ceilings or enclose it with high windows tucked up into eaves or skylights cut into our roofs. Or we can close our eyes and imagine it, bask in it, and appreciate its myriad forms of precipitation as rain, snow, sleet, or hail falls from sky into sea and evaporates back to sky once more. Perhaps the most enchanted element of any garden is a reflecting pool. When its waters lie perfectly still, it mirrors the sky; when raindrops fall, a liquid unity is created between the archetypes sky and sea.

Understanding and working with these archetypal vantage points can help us create magic lands. By asking ourselves where we want to be in any scenario, we can not only imagine, but also *know* how good it feels to sit under a certain tree or up in a tree house or out at the end of a bluff: we feel as though we have been in such a setting—in its archetypal form—before. Being able to model our feelings based on "reading" a landscape helps us move through space with familiarity and ease; it also helps us make insightful decisions about our environment: where to pitch the tent, locate the terrace, even choose what the most auspicious site might be for a new house.

One quick scan and we can sense from past experience when a cave-like setting feels too confining or a promontory-like place feels too scary, and we can move on to more secure territory. At the same time, we intuitively place ourselves in vantages that feel good, choosing the booth in the bar or the corner table in the restaurant where we feel backed up while surveying the world around us.

The seven archetypes help you begin to see the world as a garden, offering a vocabulary that describes a set of forms that you feel strongly about. Are you a sea person—someone who loves to be surrounded by softness? Or a cave person—someone who needs little huts for nestling? Or a harbor person—someone who requires a clearly defined space around you? Are you a promontory person—do you need the exhilaration of living at the edge all the time? Or an islander—someone who loves to feel independent and free? Are you a mountain person—one who sits high up with a long perspective over the world? Or a sky person—someone who lives in the "ozone," or in a constant euphoric state. Knowing who you are in terms of your landscape ideal tells you much about yourself and your "place in the world." It offers you confidence that *you* can create a place that feels like home: a space that you already know, in terms of its elements, its qualities, even its dimensions. Feel this confidence as you read. For without thinking directly about it, you are already making good decisions about the design of your garden.

EXERCISE: ARCHETYPAL VANTAGES

Think about the archetypal vantages in your house, apartment, or garden—the places that you always sit for comfort, for contemplation, for romance. List them: the window seat looking out over the park, the shower that offers you a daily chance to immerse yourself, the daybed that feel like a sleigh in the corner of your family room, a dark and cozy inglenook, the little viewing balcony onto the living room, the hammock strung between two pines, the boulder that the kids climb on, the grape arbor covered with vines.

Now imagine creating new vantages. Where would they be and how would they feel? Could you make a cozy conversation area in a corner by the wood stove? Or install a hot tub for gazing at the stars on cold winter nights? Or create a grove of your favorite trees, in an underused part of your yard? Or place a round terrace in the center of your lawn? What about turning a hall into a one-person library? Or making a music room, for performing or for listening? Knowing how to construct places that make you feel good is the first step in creating your magic land.

Chapter 3

Enchanted Landscapes

The natural landscape holds resonant images for each of us.

GARDEN is a place to grow things: roses; vegetables; trees, shrubs, and flowers, arranged in formal or informal beds and borders. The formal garden sets itself apart from the natural landscape through the use of geometric patterns and through symmetry. A garden can also work *with* the landscape rather than set itself apart. By using curved lines and asymmetric placement, you follow the more natural patterns of the earth. In an informal garden there may be an array of open and closed, dark and light, small and large spaces that derive their inspiration from Mother Earth. It is useful to explore the enchantment of natural landscapes and distill the images that speak to us; we can use them to create the same magic in our gardens.

I have always been someone who literally quivers with joy when I find a landscape that appeals to me. My daughter Lindsey shares this trait. When she was just four years old, we spent a month on an old farm in Devon, England. Every day, we'd walk a different part of its 700-acre grounds. Her favorite jaunt was a trail through a wetland meadow that took us down stone steps, across a wooden bridge over a brook, and up again through a grove of ancient beech trees. Whenever I would ask her, "Shall we take the 'Meadow Garden Walk' today?" Lindsey would smile a secret smile and give a little shiver of delight. And off we'd go.

I too get shivery every morning on my ritual walk with the dogs. My favorite route is the one that takes me through our suburban neighborhood streets and down a dark lane to a hillside meadow protected by the town as conservation land. No matter how many times I do this walk, I continue to get excited about the same things: the tunnel-like narrow lane rimmed by ancient hemlock trees; the tiny stone pump house that nestles against a flowing stream; the huge oak tree that leans alone out over the meadow; the winding path that leads up the hill to an old oak and hickory forest; and the park bench under the trees that feels as if it had been placed there just for me.

Our experience of a landscape is made up of a number of different landforms: hills and dales, rivers and ponds, forests and meadows. If you study these features and understand how and why they make you feel the way they do, then you can use them in your garden designs. This chapter describes some of these patterns on the land and suggests ways that you might apply them to your garden to make it the richer realm that it deserves to be.

EXERCISE: EXPLORE NATURE

If you want to design a garden, it helps to go directly to the source: Nature herself. There you can learn the answer to many

* * * * *

The park bench under the trees feels as if it had been placed there just for me.

aesthetic, philosophical, and technical questions. How do you set rocks along a stream so that they look natural? Study a riverscape, where you will learn about how erosion and deposition along the bank determine rock placement; how slowly water moves in a wide shallow pool versus its speed in a narrow deep channel. You can learn how to construct a waterfall with a "falling stone" set between two higher flanking stones, and how to riffle water to create wonderful sounds. From walking in a forest, you can learn how far apart to plant trees to allow in dappled sunlight, and you can study the habits and location of mosses and ferns in a woodland setting. If you live on a dry sunny slope, you can find a similar environment in nature and study which plants survive there and how they look in the wild. By connecting directly with the world of nature, you find pleasure—and design ideas—all around you.

WILDERNESS

Every home needs a wild place, especially if young children live there. My favorite haunts growing up were the edges of our property and those farther off that we didn't own at all, the unkempt scruffy thickets where adventures were sure to occur. In our "wilderness," we harvested chicory and made "coffee," discovered baby rabbits, made grassy beds, and constructed stick forts and lived in them for the day.

The grand dame of garden design, Rosemary Verey, created a wilderness at Barnsley House in the Cotswolds. According to Mrs.

Verey, everyone needs a space "where you can walk and sit and feel alone with nature. It should be a quiet and shady place, with mown paths winding between ornamental trees and shrubs, and flowers studding the grass. A wilderness fulfills these requirements."[1]

A wilderness was often created as a feature of eighteenth-century English gardens. Irregular paths that meandered through a wood were created as a natural antidote to the more rigidly formal and open garden layouts of the era, supplying the need for enclosed, canopied areas where voyagers might experience the fearful delight of feeling lost—or, in archetypal terms: finding themselves immersed. Hermitages and huts, springs and water channels, and sometimes grottoes, ruins, and even an artificial volcano were built to induce intense feelings in visitors, who could safely experience nature in all its seeming wildness. Imagine the wonder of such a wilderness in a day of strict manners and courtly behavior! How else in civilized society could one experience the anxiety of becoming lost in a forest— while feeling safe within the confines of a garden enclosure?

The "wild garden" eventually came to replace the wilderness as a place for the cultivation of plants found in the wild, especially native species or those particular to the conditions of the place, such as wetlands or desert plants. This movement first arose in nineteenth-century England when designers sought to develop gardens in wild settings like gorges, chalk pits, and quarries, and then to plant them with naturalized tangles of vegetation, rather than the smoothly grassed, carefully groomed landscape parks that had been popular the century before. Later, William Robinson and Gertrude Jekyll began a movement to naturalize flowers in grassy slopes and shady woodlands, mingling natives with exotic plantings throughout the

---

[1] Rosemary Verey. *Rosemary Verey's Making of a Garden*. London: Frances Lincoln Ltd., 1995, p. 133.

garden. Both designers felt that plants should grow so as to appear natural, creating a garden scene of character and beauty.

Using indigenous plantings that naturally flourish in your particular environment will tend to require less maintenance than if you use their more cultured and hybridized counterparts. But watch out: Some of them may overrun your garden completely while other more tender natives may need special attention. Match your soil and weather conditions with the natives that you want to use. Wetland plants, for example, must be planted in a well-watered environment; the same conditions might drown a drought-tolerant plant. And don't forget that all plants, native or cultivated, will require sufficient water and regular maintenance to survive.

If nothing else, a wilderness can be thought of as an "undesigned" part of the garden, a catchall where you put all the trees and shrubs that you've always wanted to own but can't find a place for. How wonderful to own a wilderness — especially one that is full to the brim with beloved plants.

EXERCISE: INGREDIENTS FOR A HEALTHY GARDEN

What are the ingredients necessary to making a healthy garden? First, you need to know about the growing conditions on your land. Second, you must be prepared to ameliorate those conditions where possible, or find plants that can accept the conditions that you have. Third, you need to be ruthlessly honest in assessing your own strengths and limitations about owning and keeping a garden. Let's take them one at a time:

First, learn the conditions of your land: Figure out where the sunny and shady parts of the garden are in the different seasons, where the land is boggy or dry, and which direction the winds come from in summer and in winter. Making charts or diagrams containing this information will ensure that you don't ignore it as you place your plantings: Putting tender plants in the path of a severe winter wind from the northeast will surely kill them, just as placing shade-loving plants in the full sun or wet-footed plants in dry shade will.

Second, choose plants that match your conditions, or if possible, improve the conditions to match the plantings that you desire. Perhaps the single most important ingredient to creating a beautiful and healthy garden is good soil. I've learned the hard way over the years that plants repay your investment in them manyfold if you give them the best possible growing medium from the start and continue to improve it every year. The goal is to create a soil that nourishes the roots of your plants and allows air in and water out. Depending on where you live and the materials that are available, you can choose to add nutrients to your existing soil or bring in ready-made dirt or compost and spread it over your beds.

Finally, think carefully about how much time and money you can really afford to spend on your garden. Few garden books talk about the expenses of creating and maintaining a garden—but I know I am always shocked each year at how much I've spent on topsoil, compost, mulch, tools, and structural items that are necessary in order to even begin to plant. Any stone or brickwork—the bones of a garden— can add up to hundreds of dollars in materials alone, not to mention any labor that you hire out. Plants, the obsession of most gardeners, inevitably add up quickly, especially when you order from catalogs in the doldrums of winter or visit garden centers in the first thralls of spring.

Time is another magic ingredient of garden making, because nothing will get done without it. Be realistic about how much time you can devote to your garden daily, weekly, or even seasonally. Don't create a high-maintenance perennial border if you only have an hour a week to weed, water, and stake. Don't create a wildflower meadow that blooms throughout the summer if you won't be there to enjoy it. Many gardening books are devoted to gardening techniques for easy maintenance—find them and read them carefully.

As stewards of our little piece of Mother Earth for a short period of her existence, we must learn to live lightly and garden responsibly. We can improve the conditions that we find and grow plants that will flourish in them; we can be conscious of and careful about our use of scarce resources like water, and refrain as far as possible from using toxic materials such as pesticides, herbicides, and chemical fertilizers that hurt our water, soils, and air. With an understanding of these main ingredients, we can nurture and preserve the magic land that, in turn, nurtures us all— Mother Earth.

ENCHANTED FORESTS AND GARDEN GROVES

A trip to New Zealand a few years back brought our family in contact with a true forest primeval: the rain forest. How beautiful it was: Tree ferns growing out of beds of mosses topped by stands of false beech trees towering over the cool damp atmosphere of utter greenness. Meandering streams further lubricated the already glistening ground; narrow wooden bridges enticed the visitor to continue the voyage into the depths of this venerable landscape. The forest's stillness seemed to whisper, creating the sense of a secret language that the rustling leaves and the winging birds all spoke with delicacy. We were intruders in a magic land that resembled my image of heaven.

I have had other "woods" experiences that have touched my soul as deeply. Hunting for bamboo shoots in the middle of a timber bamboo forest in Japan, I was mesmerized by the swishes and clucks of the supple trunks as their leafy manes caught the wind like sails. Or in England, suddenly happening upon a bluebell wood whose celestial brilliance lit up the naked trunks of beech trees. Or in Bali, being led into a jungle lit only by the light of the full moon to attend a puppet theater festival that lasted until dawn. Or closer to home, walking my dogs down an oak and beech forest path and watching the light, the colors, the canopy alter, reflecting the season's change. I know that I long for forests and that I have needed to create at least one little garden grove on my half acre to satisfy my sylvan remembrances.

Think back to some of your favorite forest experiences. Even a small stand of trees can excite associations of woodsy wanderings: following animal tracks to a hollowed-out tree; making stick forts in the gnarly roots of an ancient oak; crouching low under pine boughs to watch the chipmunks burrow under a thick blanket of needles.

Remember some of your favorite children's stories—so many were set in enchanted forests, remote woods, or sylvan settings. This summer, I was one of three adults who plotted a trail through a dense thicket of woodland, and then proceeded to lop, clip, prune, and saw away branches so that people could enter the forest to appreciate its beauty. We created a meandering path system that took members of the adjacent church and their children into a part of the property that no one used. We cleared brush, left logs for sitting benches, formalized a large clearing for an outdoor chapel, and created natural passageways for neighbors to stroll through the forest. We felt like ten-year-olds—all excited about opening and revealing the treasures of this woodland and getting sweaty and dirty in the process. We'll continue to work on it next summer until it begins to fit our vision of what this forest garden should be.

A forest on a small property? It doesn't sound possible. Yet there is no rule that states that a garden must be always open to the sky. If you want a grovelike feeling on your land, then you will need to plant trees, and lots of them. One client wanted a Japanese-style garden for her 25 × 60-foot urban lot. We created a rivulet with a low waterfall that curved through a perfect little forest. We installed a total of twenty-five trees, including cedars, cryptomerias, hollies, hinoki cypresses, cherries, magnolias, and Japanese maples, to give the effect of wandering through a delightful garden grove. With so many trees in such a small area, the effect was magical: It felt as though an enchanted forest had always been there.

A forest in a garden is really a grove, a small wood without underbrush. The memories we have of forests are really of groves, for the scrubby, often-ugly undergrowth of brambles and bittersweet, tangles and thickets and scrubby growth that one finds in "real" forests are cleaned up in the imagination, just as a garden

orest in a garden is really a grove, a small wood without underbrush. The memories we have of forests • really of groves.

grove is. Not all groves need to mimic the natural landscape: They can be geometric in character as well. Orchards, plantations, *allées*, and bosques are all collections of trees planted in strict formation. Creating a geometric grove can be magical as well.

With small spaces and tight budgets, most people cannot imagine planting a grove of trees in their backyard landscapes. Yet owning a group of stately trees is akin to possessing a collection of priceless jewels: They only grow in value and in stature over time. Think about a place to plant a grove and then decide what kind of grove it should be: plants of the same species such as a grouping of cherries, an orchard of apple trees, a stand of birches. Or perhaps the grove should be a mixture of needle leaf and deciduous trees, placed to block a view of the neighbor's house. With a big budget, you can buy large trees from the start, then arrange them so that they offer an ever-changing focal screen. Or plant small and wait.

CLEARINGS, DELLS, AND GLADES

Sometimes, when you are wandering in a forest, you come suddenly upon a "clearing," a tract of land cleared of wood and brush, a sunlit area open to the sky. Its brightness stands in stark contrast to the surrounding darkness, and its light nurtures a different set of plants from its surrounds. These magic openings help us imagine how to structure our gardens as enchanted lands.

Think about your own house and its original setting. It is likely that a forest was cleared in order to build your home. If you are lucky, your contractor left fringes of trees between houses to provide privacy and to mark lot lines. In such a case, your house already sits in the middle of a clearing. If it doesn't, you may find it helpful to imagine replacing the surrounding scrub, bush, or veldt with more ornamental trees, shrubs, and ground covers.

A "dell" is a small, secluded, natural hollow or valley, usually covered with trees, turf, or ground cover—often of a single species. Lately, I've been walking past such a dell every day. Carved out by the glaciers 10,000 years ago, this little valley faces north, is roofed over by spindly white pine trees, and is carpeted with pine needles. I wouldn't have noticed it except that it forms a discreet and private little hollow in the land, a place in which you could nestle if you required protection in a storm. In the spring, I imagine that little plants will emerge from under their sparse winter blanket, stretching upward to the baffled light. What will they be? Will there be enough light to birth ferns, partridgeberry, wood anemone, or lady's slippers?

On the south side of my house, under a stand of tall maples and oaks, I am preparing beds for a fern dell. Here I hope to collect and display as many species of hardy ferns as I can find. I've placed a twig bench and set out the stepping-stones already. I am now ready to plant in this area of dappled sun and leafy boughs. My favorite dell ever, however, is one that I cannot reproduce: a glowworm dell in New Zealand. This vertical landscape was a cavelike hollow at the bottom of high fern-clad cliff walls down which trickles of water fell to create a moist, dark place where the *Arachnocampa* congregate, gnats whose larvae possess bioluminescent excretory organs and spin sticky webs in order to attract food insects. Their tiny flickering lights, accompanied by the soft splashing of water on rock and the mysteries of the depths of night, created an unforgettable magic land for my family and for me.

A "glade" is another kind of open space surrounded by woods. Its archaic meaning is an open stretch or group of interconnected openings forming a passage through a woodland. In my garden, I have two areas as glades. My front garden is a glade formed around an oval lawn where my daughter Charlotte's garden lies. Together we've planted compact box hedges in a zigzag design to either side of the front walk and cultivated the old-fashioned perennials that she loves—foxgloves, lupine, columbine, peonies, and standard roses along the privet hedge on the street side. In the backyard is another grassy glade ringed by trees, in this case a much larger play space for bocce, croquet, and badminton, around which are planted perennials and shrubs topped with towering old oaks, hemlocks, and white pines. Glades, dells, and clearings can be wonderful organizing ideas for your garden, as they have been for mine.

MEADOWS

A "meadow" is an open tract of low-lying, often level grassland. It is open to the sun, exposed to the wind, and usually expansive in extent: a wildflower meadow of Queen Anne's Lace and black-eyed Susans; a manicured lawn strewn with miniature English daisies; a field of red poppies near the land of Oz; a pasture or a prairie, a moor or a marsh; a savanna or a veldt.

Whenever I see a meadow, I long to lie on my back in the middle of it. I am not alone. We have a tendency to seek out the center of a flat open space. Perhaps it speaks to our innate search for secure places. A farmer, on hearing me speak of this phenomenon, told me of a round field that he mows in the spring, starting from the outer edge and spiraling inward. He never finishes the job without stopping his machine just short of the center, where he often finds a nest of newborn fawns, abandoned temporarily by a helpless doe. He imagines that she chooses this spot because she can survey her entire environment, so when her babies are old enough, they can sense danger and flee from it. In our gardens, we use the center of a lawn to set out focal points such as a birdbath, statue, or reflecting pool, or we choose to create a basking place for ourselves in the sun.

A prairie is bigger than a meadow. Settlers arriving in America's heartland 150 years ago described a "sea of grass" in their journals, where tall-grass prairie covered 30 million acres of land in Iowa alone. Big bluestem grass rose eight feet high, interspersed with black-eyed Susans, purple coneflowers, and other natives, such as "prairie smoke" or "rattlesnake master." Today, nearly all of the Iowa prairie is gone, plowed under to create farmlands of corn and soybeans. But in that state and in other midwestern American and Canadian states, the prairie restoration movement is going strong. Refuges are being established where grasses can grow without threat of mowing, and wildlife—including butterflies, birds, and even buffalo—are returning to the land. Prairie education centers continue horticultural research and teach children about ecological issues and the life cycle of prairies. Books and courses on how to create prairie gardens are popular, helping homeowners bring the beauties of prairie flowers into their neighborhoods and onto their properties.[2]

ROCKERIES

I am completely in love with stone.

I can date this obsession back to my youth, when we would play in a forest preserve near our house. Our favorite place was the old stone foundation of a house, complete with blackened fireplace and crumbling chimney still standing. Big old oak trees rose high over the ruin, their leaves creating a soft, spongy surface underfoot. I was fascinated by the stones' story: Where had they come from? Who had placed them? What family had lived within these walls? I always felt that if the rocks could talk, they would have long sagas to recite.

My apprenticeship in Japan only fueled my passion for stone. In Kyoto, I studied, built, and tried to design Japanese gardens, but my greatest learning took place when I followed my garden master into the field to watch him set rocks. His hands like a conductor's, his

[2]Mike Krapfl. "Creating a Sea of Grass," *American Way,* 15 April 1997, p. 74.

face set quietly in easy concentration, he would guide each stone into place with effortless grace. He would place a rock on the right side of the garden, then balance it with one on the left, then one in the center, and so on; never "finishing" one composition until the whole felt in equilibrium.

I finally got my turn to set rocks a few years later, in a home built on the edge of a quarry in—appropriately enough—Rockport, Massachusetts. The client had commissioned a Japanese-style garden from a contractor, and what he had received were two egg-shaped mounds with rocks sticking out of them. Clearly, the man had had no image for what he was trying to create and no sense of how rocks wanted to sit in the ground. With a different—and sympathetic—contractor, I began to build my first garden. I chose to create three icons of traditional garden making: the "tortoise island," the "crane island," and the "dry waterfall," and off I went. My first night after setting some twenty rocks, I was euphoric. I knew that I was meant to be a garden designer. All night long, I couldn't stop thinking about the rocks and, according to my husband, even tried to direct the eaves into place as we lay sleeping in our attic room.

ROCK SETTING

Once you know some basic principles of rock setting, you can apply this information to creating natural rockeries in your own landscape. First, learn something about the geology of the stones in your area. Igneous rocks such as granite and diorite are formed by the solidification of magma in the earth; sedimentary rocks such as limestone and shale are formed by fragments transported from their source and deposited elsewhere by water; and metamorphic rocks such as schist or gneiss are formed by a pronounced change created by pressure, heat, or water that results in a more compact and more highly crystalline condition. I find that the igneous and metamorphic rocks tend to be the most versatile for rock setting; their beautiful veining, colors, and striations offer many choices to the designer as to their use. I especially use granites, also gneisses and schists when available, to create Japanese-style gardens, to make waterfalls, and to edge ponds and as benches in informal settings. Limestone, with its horizontal layering, must be placed parallel to the ground, just as it was formed, and so is useful for creating ledge outcroppings on a hillside, but not for vertical accents in a garden.

What if you don't have indigenous rocks to work with? First, call your local gravel yards and nurseries to find out their sources for stone. If there seems to be no one who is able to supply you locally, there are rock farms that will ship boulders, smaller stones, and gravel anywhere in the country, for a price, of course. Don't accept blasted rocks, because the sharp edges and shards are not only unaesthetic to see, but also dangerous to brush against. And be careful not to choose too many different types of stone for one garden area—colors can be jarring and textures inharmonious.

Once, on a rock shopping expedition with a client in Milwaukee, we came across three stones embedded with seams of amethyst! Rather than setting them with the other limestone ledges we were creating, which would have looked strange, we placed them apart from the rest: a triad of very special stones that one came upon just after crossing through the garden gate.

Once you get a pile of stones amassed, how do you go about setting them? First, decide what you are trying to create: a rocky hillside for alpine plantings, a backyard rill, a pond and waterfall, or perhaps a dry landscape in the Japanese style.

Next, choose a focal stone—usually the largest or most interesting—and decide how you want to set it. Think about whether it is best suited to be a standing stone, a lying stone, a sitting stone, or one that is set on a diagonal. Notice the marks that indicate where it

Often stones look best set as they were by Mother Nature herself.

sat while in the ground: Often stones look best set as they were by Mother Nature herself.

Now think about the rock in anthropomorphic terms: Where is its head, its foot, its front, and its back? How much do you need to bury it so that it feels well set, balanced, and secure in the earth? One rule of thumb: Never place a rock so that you can see underneath it—it looks precarious, or tossed, rather than carefully set. It should always sit solidly in the earth.

Is the rock to be placed as a lone specimen or part of a larger grouping? If the former, then make sure that the focal rock feels balanced by others nearby. If a grouping, then think about placing smaller rocks at the foot of the focal rock to "support" it. Sometimes I think about stones as little vignettes of pleasurable experiences: A large stone with a small stone I think of as a "mother and child" grouping; three stones might represent cows grazing, islands upon a sea, or the Buddhist triad—with Buddha at the center and two disciples at each foot. In Japan, we were taught to place stones in arrangements of three, five, and seven rocks respectively, to give a sense of asymmetry and imperfection that mimics stones as they are seen in nature.

Use plants that are in scale with the rocks to soften and enhance them. Mosses, ferns, alpines, heathers and heaths, and ornamental grasses all look wonderful in a stone garden, as do small-scale azaleas and low-growing junipers. Just as stones form the bedrock—the skeletal structure—of our earth, so too can they form the bones of our gardens.

Chapter 4

Your Enchanted Home

Begin to see your home as a garden.

Y daughter Charlotte and I play a game whenever we get in a car together. We drive along and point out the houses that look "happy." "There's a happy house," she will exclaim. I'll look quickly as I drive past and agree. "What about that one?" I will ask. "Smiley," she'll reply as she sees a little white cape with dark green shingles and a red door. "How about that one? Happy?" I'll ask. "No, bored," she'll assert as we drive past a brick Tudor with white trim, little landscaping, and no detailing to speak of. As we pass by another taupe-colored Victorian, complete with turret, large colonnaded front porch, and red door and trim, she exclaims, "Happy!"

What is your house's "happiness quotient?" When you walk outside and view your house from the street, how does it look? How welcoming to strangers? Does it appear shy? Standoffish? Or exuberant and embracing? We've decided that it isn't the size of a house or the tidiness of its yard, or the obvious manifestations of wealth that makes a house seem happy. Sometimes the most intriguing houses are snug, cozy little cottages, or ones strewn with playthings in their front yard, or those that need a new coat of paint. Some of the most unhappy are new, oversized "trophy" houses that occupy most of the space on a small site. How do you create a happy home for yourself and your loved ones?

A house, after all, is a symbol of your self and the "self" of your family. Think of the front of your house as being like a person's face (thus "façade"). You can then begin to perceive what makes a house seem happy from the outside. In the same way you gauge people's emotions from the expression on their faces (a scowl, an upturned eyebrow, wide-eyed), people will view the "expression" of your house to determine its being. The roof is like a hat on the head of the house: It can sit as a peaked hat pulled low over the house to protect it from the elements; or perch sedately like your mother's pillbox hat of yore. Our house's red-tiled roof slopes asymmetrically down low over the stucco façade, so it looks like a German hunting lodge set deep within the Black Forest.

The windows of a house are its eyes—their size, number, and divisions directly affect the appearance of the facade. Undivided windows seem to be giving the world an unblinking stare; mullioned windows tend to break up light and break down the breadth of the opening into smaller fragments. Also, changing a window's style, size, shutter details, or glass type makes a big difference in the way that you read a facade.

The front door is, of course, the mouth. You move through it to gain entry. The color, size, and thickness of the door and its hardware and fenestration is designed to beckon you in or to keep you out. Our thick oak door has no window in it, but instead has a small opening with grillwork for shooting arrows at marauding hordes as they ride by. Not a very welcoming front door, but very protective indeed!

The details of a house can make a huge difference. When you first view your house and add all the "special effects," you should get a sense of it as a shelter. Some of the things we've noticed over our years of house viewing: cream colors, warm hues, and saturated colors all seem to suggest a happy household within. Cool colors such as blues and greens are more standoffish unless deep and full-bodied in tone. We've rarely seen a happy house that has too much trim on it, and as long as they harmonize, we find that the more colors used the better. Hand-carved or handmade details delight: Our house hosts a concrete frieze of a profile of a wild boar rosette underscored by the date "1507." Visitors scratch their heads about the age of our house, amazed by its good condition, until they realize that the Pilgrims hadn't even arrived at Plymouth Rock yet!

Unhappiness is evident when a place is unkempt or neglected. The result is a home that feels forlorn, saddened, or depressed. The act of attending to one's home can help bring happiness into your life, so your house becomes a true symbol of the evolution of your state of mind. If you think of turning your house into a magic land, by working on the outside or on the inside, you will find that you can't help but bring joy into your life and into the lives of your loved ones.

THE FRONT YARD

Most people assume that a front yard is a space that should feel exposed to view for all who pass—a democratic place that is "open to the public" and closed to private activities. This view is beginning to change as lot sizes shrink and garden space becomes more valuable. You need to think of your front yard as a front garden.

Go out and take a fresh look at the front of your house. What do you see? It might be a perfectly kept lawn with plantings along the foundation and a straight and simple path running from street to house. A picket-fenced enclosure with a graceful old tree that shades the front porch in summer. A winding driveway that circles around big old shrubs to a house hidden from view by an ancient grove of trees. A high stucco wall topped with embedded glass shards and no view onto the house itself. A vibrant cottage garden dripping with annuals, perennials, vegetables, and grasses that have nearly choked out the winding path that runs through it. Or do you see a newly bulldozed site that is waiting for "landscaping," with nary a tree still left standing?

Front yards can look like any of these images and a host of others, depending on climate, culture, security concerns, and the amount of available space. But the prevailing image of the American front yard is the first and the last one: unoccupied green space that seems without character or horticultural or spatial interest. Today's owners seem to put time, effort, and dollars into their houses, with little left for their landscapes.

Perhaps you live in a neighborhood where every front yard looks the same. Perhaps you have poured time and effort into your back yard while placing a few foundation plantings around the front. If your front yard looks bland, unkempt, boring, obvious, conformist, or uninspired, then read on. You can take the opportunity to release your personality into your land by making it reflect more of who you are.

One of my favorite houses when I was growing up was a place we called the "Witch's House"—a half-timbered structure crowned with a wonderful roof that curved into a swoop at the eaves and looked like an oversized hat. It had a high hedge that was trimmed in curves and swoops to match the eaves line and that you couldn't see over to know what was actually contained in its front garden unless you peered through the peephole in the craftsman-style wooden gate. We always begged my mother to drive by again and

...e of my favorite houses when I was growing up was a place we called the "Witch's House" —
...alf-timbered structure crowned with a wonderful roof that looked like an oversized hat.

again so we could look at it. Whoever lived there, in this wild house located in a well-to-do suburban community with small lots and plenty of center-entrance colonials surrounding it, had guts to set themselves apart with such aplomb. I always imagined the place to be overrun with trick-or-treaters at Halloween.

Consider setting up a table and chairs in a sunny corner of broadleaf shrubs that you plant *in the front yard* so you can invite passing neighbors for a spot of tea. If you've got a good exposure to the sun, why not plant raised beds filled with your favorite flowers for cutting to bring inside, relating your front garden to the garden you create within the walls of your house? Or how about filling up the lawn with a mosaic of flat fieldstone and low-growing ground covers that can be a scented terrace for visitors to enjoy as a meandering front-entrance walk? But some of my favorite houses are those I can't even see, because they are set back behind a thick stand of trees that block any good view of them, leaving me to imagine what they really look like.

Anything that you think of for your back garden can be created in the front; the rules are the same. You'll need to think about all the same elements of design just as you would for any other garden. The difference is that others will see your handiwork, so how much privacy or publicity you feel comfortable with becomes an important issue in a front garden's design.

YOUR GARDEN IS NOT A YARD

yard [Old English for *geard* enclosure, yard] 1: a small enclosed area open to the sky and adjacent to a building; 2: the grounds of a building; 3: an enclosure for livestock; 4: an area set aside for a particular business or activity; 5: a system of railroad tracks for storing cars and making up trains.

Not a very magical set of images—a yard! So do like the British and think of your home's landscape not as a "yard," but as a "garden." If you start to call your front yard a "front garden," you may find that it begins to become one more quickly and easily than if you continue to call it (and therefore think of it) as a "yard." Same goes for the back "garden!"

INSIDE THE ENCHANTED HOME

A house should have a range of spaces to fit the different moods of its occupants. The archetypal places in your house—the little cavelike den in the basement, the inglenook by the fire, the balcony perched over the living room, the glassed-in porch, or the attic— each offer evocative vantage points. Rooms with special architectural features—a window seat, dormers, the rounded walls of a turret, or a leaded-glass window wall, are all places that draw people to them as points of focus in a room. A home should include a range of retreat spaces alongside its social spaces. A dark, book-lined library that sits just off the bright kitchen/family room allows those in a contemplative mood to coexist with those in a more communal state of mind. A warm and loving home provides spaces for all the different interests of its inhabitants. A music room or area, an art studio, a bar for dance, a workshop in the basement, and plenty of books permit a range of activities to take place within the home. But perhaps my favorite metaphor for a home is to think of it as a garden.

We made our house into a garden when we built a large addition onto it. We pushed out to our garage, perched at the eastern edge of our site, and built a family room, kitchen, and dining area. To contrast with the rest of our house, we decided to create a light-filled

Why not take a bright corner of your living room and make it into a garden?

pavilion-like addition. We painted each wall a different, saturated color: azure blue on the east wall, forest green on the north wall, and orange yellow on the south wall. Its cathedral ceilings are opened to the light by high porthole windows that capture glimpses of the daytime and evening skies. Plants thrive in this garden room and with the sounds of a babbling indoor fountain and four birds (two parakeets, a finch, and a lustily singing canary), it is a happy place indeed. A menagerie of animals also occupies the space: Our two dogs, two cats, and bunny rabbit all roam freely, always ready to play with our three children.

What if you live in an apartment with no outside space at all? Why not take a bright corner of your living room and make it into a garden? Surround your couch with indoor plants set up on stands so they arch around the back and side of the sofa like a garden hedge. Add garden furniture—wicker and wrought iron—to adorn different corners of the room. For extra sensory enjoyment, consider suspending wind chimes from the ceiling or importing a Victorian birdcage with your favorite species flitting and chirping within. Or employ one or a series of fish tanks as focus for the "garden" and include a small indoor fountain to aerate the air and provide auditory pleasure. Grow bulbs in two-week intervals so you always have their scent and color to enjoy. Find wonderful rugs or Oriental carpets that create garden designs on the floor. By turning your apartment or house into a magic land, you create for yourself a sensuous haven in an alien world.

PART TWO

Making Gardens

H ere, at the midpoint of my life, I create places of enchantment and dreams for others. To do it, I don work boots and travel to dusty sites and help turn the land of my clients into something magic. Making a garden that begins in one's heart, creating an image of it in one's mind, and then building it so that one can plant in it, play in it, be in it—this is wonderful work indeed!

After all these years of trial and error, I find that if I can understand what each different element of a garden means and how it functions, then I can better assemble them in a coherent and appropriate form. Therefore, I always consider the lay of the land, enclosures of sheltering arms, planting palettes, patterns on the earth, and journey making to create a good garden. Beyond these elements, I use some basic design principles to help me compose so that the garden possesses a sense of dynamic balance. In the end, it may be my ability to "hear the stream with open eyes" that brings the whole into harmony.

Gardening and garden design are arts that improve with age: the age of the gardener—experience; the age of the garden—maturity; and the age of the earth—wisdom. When involved with such work, you continue to learn; you are never finished creating and certainly never done gardening—there is always another seed germinating, plant to stake, tree limb to prune, bed to weed and mulch. I figure that by the time I'm ninety, I'll be really good at this work, sowing the seeds and planting the stones of gardens wherever I wander.

Chapter 5

Designing the Dream

Transform your garden into reality with a five-step process.

HE process of building a garden is like making magic. You transform one thing into another: A bright cloth becomes a multicolored canary; a hat houses a rabbit; a hollow becomes a wildflower dell; a stepping-stone path turns into a mountain trail; a patch of dirt sprouts a sea of color. In a garden, something is often created from nothing: Snowdrops emerge unscathed somehow from the depths of a winter mulch; fern fronds unfurl in the bony soil of pine forests; a child builds a tree fort from boughs torn down by heavy spring snows. Nature is magic and you are a magician who, with a certain verve and sleight of hand, can create a beautiful landscape out of a dull backyard. Now you see it, now you don't. Presto—a garden!

What are the steps you need to take to actually make a garden? First, you need to understand your land—to walk it with a sense of wonder. Second, you need to conjure a vision in your mind's eye.

Third, you should mock up your ideas to see whether they suit the intended situation. Fourth, you start building the bones of the garden, working in layers from the ground up. Fifth, you will need to tweak your garden, add to it, subtract from it, and keep changing it over time, until it becomes synonymous with your dream. Each step offers you the chance to enhance or alter your design as you build, so you continue to *feel* the form as you create it and *know* that it is right.

WALK YOUR LAND WITH A SENSE OF WONDER

Your land is your spiritual home on this earth. When you own property, you become its steward, responsible for keeping it healthy, nurtured, and loved. It is also your responsibility to understand its qualities, its history, its structures, and its special features. Your land, no matter how big or how small, possesses something magical about it. Perhaps it is the huge white oak that dominates the middle of the property. Or the patch of wildflower meadow that has seeded itself into existence. Or the tumble-down playhouse that sits in a scrubby corner of the lot. The magic can be found in the vantage of the site, the lay of the land, the design of the house, or the undisturbed areas around the property. You must walk your land with a sense of wonder—an open mind—and you will find clues to the design of your garden.

One of the ways to do this is to learn everything you can about your property. When was it first built? By whom? What changes were made to the house and the land? What is the geological history of the area and your site in particular? What kind of trees do you own and how old are they? What is the orientation of the site? Its prevailing winds? Its sunny spots and shady spots? For example, if you own an old farmhouse, you'll want to learn about the layout of the original farmland. Where were the gardens? The outbuildings? The orchard? You might ask yourself if there is anything you can bring back, rebuild, or restore. Gather as much information about your land as you can before you start to design.

Ask yourself what it is that you love most about your landscape. What features do you exclaim over? Play up these special elements and make them even more evident—build your whole garden around them. Do you have a "cosmic tree" on your land—a massive copper beech tree, a graceful live oak, a windblown mesquite? Or perhaps you have a superb view—of the nearby city, a distant mountain, or the sun setting in the west. Such *exclamation points* can become the magical focus of your garden.

CONJURE THE VISION

Once you've identified the exclamation points of your site, you now need to conjure up one or a variety of possible landscape scenarios that feels right for your land. In other words, you have to evoke a vision. Part 1 explored a series of images that you might find helpful in determining what your garden should look and feel like. You can also try other ways of eliciting images: By flipping through garden books and magazines for ideas, you search for visual motifs to augment your base of information; by making little plans and sketches as doodles on a notepad, you try ideas on paper to see how their elements interrelate; and by daydreaming about the garden during quiet moments of the day or night, you use your imagination to test how these ideas look and feel in three dimensions. These techniques help me conjure a vision of design concepts that might work and allow me to reject ones that may not be appropriate.

You cannot design anything without a clear image in your head before you start. Finding this image may take a few short minutes or long years of searching, but realizing it is definitely worth the wait.

You suddenly realize that you want a reflecting pool in your garden to bring heaven down into it.

What happens is you begin to subconsciously sift through information to find just the right idea. Perhaps you are reading a book and a phrase jumps out at you: from Henry David Thoreau's *Walden*, for example, "Heaven is under our feet as well as over our heads." You suddenly realize that he is right— you want a reflecting pool in your garden to bring heaven down into it. Now that you have the big idea you enjoy a flooding sensation; a feeling that the idea is "just right" engulfs you. You imagine this pond in your garden, trying it in different locations in your mind's eye. You imagine how big it should be, and what rocks and plants you will place around it to fit your visual image of a reflecting pool. You will have a sense that you understand the design not only as a whole concept, but also in its various details—a euphoric feeling of certainty, of rightness, and of joy. The next step will be to test the image on your land.

THE AHA MOMENT

An "aha" moment occurs when you suddenly awaken with a great idea in your head or when you tweak something just a little so that it falls into its proper place within the design. It is a time when all the disparate forces seem to harmonize; to congeal into rightness. This happens many times throughout the design process: when you realize the right image for your garden, when you lay out just the right curve for the new stone walls, when you figure out—at last—exactly what to do in the corner by the door, when certain planting schemes flower in ways you could only dream. These are moments when the potential of your garden seems close to being realized.

I usually experience my aha moments just upon waking in the early hours of the morning. Perhaps my mind has been quietly working away on the problem all night, and I awaken with it solved. Sometimes I experience an aha moment on a walk with the dogs, or driving along the highway, or when I flip through books or magazines. An idea emerges from nowhere, it seems, and it is a good one. Then I need to give it a reality check—to mock it up, to draw it, to bring it to my collaborators who will punch holes into it. The more aha moments I experience, the more I seem to have. They are the lifeblood of the creative process.

MAKE A MOCK-GARDEN

Just because you thought up a big idea doesn't mean that it is the right one for the site. What you need to do next is to test it by drawing it or making a mock-garden in three dimensions right on the land that you intend to transform.

Most people feel uncomfortable making drawings in order to understand their ideas. But try it anyway: Quick sketches allow you to test conceptual ideas, relationships between elements, and details that might be used to carry out the design. Trying out an idea in plan view—from a bird's-eye perspective—or as a cross section or elevation, permits you to think through, and thus experience, the top, side, and front faces of any object or vignette that you can think of. Some people are skilled at creating little three-dimensional perspective sketches that allow you to feel as if you are inhabiting the idea on paper. These are skills you can learn and improve by practicing, until the ideas start to flow easily from your hand. Sketching is a wonderful tool for expressing and trying out your garden ideas before you start to build.

Another fun technique to try is making a collage that expresses how your garden will look and feel. To create one, take photographs of your land and draw over them, or find appropriate images from magazines and paste them together to simulate your garden's design. You can place words, poetry, or bars of music over the collage. The collage becomes a visual reminder of what you are aiming to accomplish in your garden and serves to keep you inspired as you build your dream.

Every chance I get I try to make a mock-up of my design concepts in three dimensions before I begin actual garden construction. No matter how well I can conjure up a design in my head, I need to see its size, shape, focal points, and general pattern outlined in front of me. For example, in trying to figure out how big a rock we needed as a new base for the twelve-foot-high Japanese lantern in Boston's Public Garden, we made a mock-lantern using a full-size blueprint mounted on cardboard and stood it on a base of boxes covered with a tarpaulin in order to view it from the different vistas around the lagoon. After adding and subtracting boxes, we determined that we needed a single flat stone measuring fifteen feet long by eight feet wide by four feet high in order for it to look right with the height of the lantern. When we finally found such a rock, it actually weighed in at eighteen tons! It took a huge hydraulic crane to install it, but it looked magnificent. Imagine our distress after *all* this if we had not made a mock-up first and had estimated the wrong size!

You can use your ingenuity when you make a mock-up of a design. Mock-stepping-stones can be made out of newsprint or cardboard, or simply drawn with a stick onto dirt. Planting beds can be outlined with hoses, rope, limestone particles, or orange spray paint (depending on the amount of permanence you are seeking). Vertical elements can be configured by using ladders, sheets, tall stakes, plywood boards, or boxes stacked on high. I often get workmen to pose as trees (arms upraised) and shrubs (crouched!) and have cut out cardboard shapes to suggest stones or statues. Once, I needed to convince a client that two large stone goat statues that he owned would fit into his small urban garden. All I had to do was to make cardboard mock-ups to size (complete with beards) and place them in his garden so he could study them at his leisure over the weekend. Monday morning he called and gave me the go-ahead. The stone goats still stand tethered in his garden today.

BUILD THE FRAME

Once you have made a mock-up of your ideas on the land, it is time to build the basic framework of your garden. Usually, this means manipulating the horizontal structure of the landscape: the hills and valleys, the walls, terraces, pathways, and ground covers; but also the vertical forms: the large trees, gateways, trellises, and fencing. It is like constructing the framework of a house around you without placing any furniture within it. You can feel its three dimensions as a pure form and can begin to understand how to flesh it out slowly over time.

To build the frame of your garden, you need to understand how each element in the garden functions—you need a perspective and approach for their design. Chapters 6 through 10 discuss these basic garden elements in some detail. I attempt to crystallize my thinking and experiences into useful ways of seeing that hopefully will facilitate your design decisions.

TWEAK THE GARDEN OVER TIME

Continually changing the look of your garden, by subtracting or adding elements, by creating new garden areas, and of course, by maintaining the whole, keeps the magic of your garden alive. Chapters 11 and 12 look at some of the principles that will help guide us in composing and reworking the magic land that we seek.

Gardens are a metaphor for life. They are planted, they grow, they change, they mature, they wither, and they die. A plant's seeds may fall on the ground and produce new progeny and so continue the life cycle on and on. The principles that can guide us in designing our garden can help us in living life. Remember that your garden has a life cycle just as you do: Pay attention and allow it to go through its own developmental stages, and allow it to thrive by attending to its needs throughout its life span.

Chapter 6

The Lay of the Land

Make your yard into a garden by sculpting your land.

ORK with your land as a sculptor. Look at it as a huge piece of clay that requires a loving hand to bring out its essential (or potential) beauty. Where a protrusion naturally occurs, give it prominence by simplifying, softening, or sharpening its form and its features. Think of a hill as a saddle, a nose, a spur, a tongue; as breasts or belly or buttocks. Where a major trough or depression occurs, exaggerate its concavity by clearing it, excavating it, or filling it with water to give it a clear bowl-like, crater-shaped, or even cavernous form. Play with your landscape; feel the lay of your land through your heart as well as through your hands. Massage your little bit of Mother Earth so her inherent grace and beauty are revealed as form and figure—as corpus—of your garden.

With this perspective in mind, think about the overall grading of your property. Do you live on a flat or a hilly site? If hilly, does your land slope downhill or uphill in relation to the house? In each of these three cases—the flat site, the uphill slope, and the downhill slope—your relationship to your garden and the land that it sits on is different.

THINK OF THE LANDSCAPE AS A BODY

Haven't you ever wanted to stroke the soft grasses of a meadow? To nestle into the folds of a valley or to lie encased within the fern-filled slopes of a deep ravine? To caress the sides of a hill? Without being entirely conscious of it, you feel a landscape as a palpable physical body whose convexities entice touch and whose concavities invite inhabitation. One way to understand your site is to view it as a sculptor does, by feeling the lay of your land.

We explore our land the way that we once explored our mother's body, feeling her voluptuous curves and her hollow cavities, her bony ridges, and her life-enhancing liquids. Land can feel swollen or parched, bumpy or pockmarked, knobby or gnarly, pitted or sunken, furrowed or notched, weather-beaten or smooth—just about anything that a human body can be. A landscape's features act as landmarks, setting apart a piece of ground as distinctive, just as beauty marks, freckles, dimples, and wrinkles render a face unique.

LEVEL LAND

Level land is both the easiest and hardest kind of site to have. Easy, because you can do almost anything you want on it, and hard because you have no limitations but your own imagination. A flat site

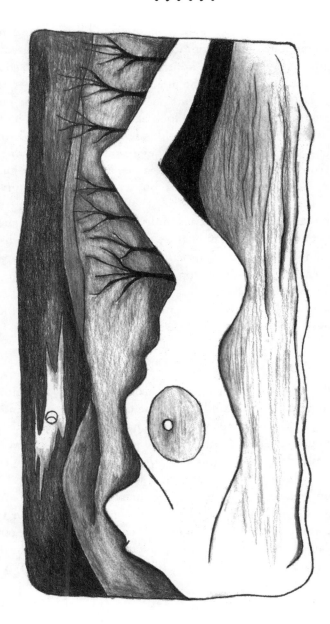

We explore our land the way that we once explored our mother's body, feeling her voluptuous curves and her hollow cavities, her bony ridges and her life-enhancing liquids.

requires vision and a firm hand; for something that is regular can only become exotic through definition and exaggeration. These days, land is usually leveled to build a housing development, sanitized of vegetation, sodded, and left for the new owner to landscape—one of the toughest garden design problems one can have. Often, the new residents are strapped for cash and look around for easy and inexpensive solutions to the landscaping dilemma. What they see is the suburban foundation planting and so they install one too, leaving a wide-open front lawn with little shrubs and spindly trees that hug the house. A waste of money, perhaps, but worse—of space and of vision.

You can really do just about anything with a flat piece of land. You can plant an orchard on it, enclose it with fences, create hills and vales upon it, make a pond or turn the whole thing into a gravel garden. You can create a formal topiary garden, an herb garden, a perennial nursery. The list is endless. What a flat site does require is a clear sense of enclosure, vantage, and organization around a focal point. I'll cover each of these design elements later in this book.

UPWARD SLOPE

When you live on a site that slopes upward, you look up and into a hillside. Your visual field is confined to the tilted-up piece of land that rises above you. This means that you have an intimate, or close-up view of your garden on a hill. This is a good condition to have, because the hillside acts as both enclosure and focal point. However, your problem will be to provide it with a sense of organization, depending on what your concept for the site might be.

You may choose from many ideas for designing your upward-sloping site. You can run water down it by creating a rill or waterfall that recirculates back upward from a pool at its feet. You might use the slope as a canvas, painting swaths of heathers, or ornamental grasses, or wildflowers in bold strokes. You could create a rockery with little stepping-stone paths and pockets of alpine plants or moss, or simply cover the whole hill with grass to create an abstract mountain in your backyard. With such an interesting draw for the eye, you should look for ways to sit at its base in order to look up into your slope garden. You could create a terrace there or nestle a bench or a viewing pavilion into the slope. In order to enhance your view onto the garden from inside the house, you might consider painting the interior window mullions a color to match your garden architecture or its plantings such as a teal blue or forest green, or choose curtains with a design that recalls the patterns created in your garden. The upward slope offers you a garden tilted backward as though on an easel—a work of art created from the materials of nature for your continual enjoyment both inside and outside the house.

DOWNWARD SLOPE

If your house sits near or at the top of a hill, the bulk of your garden will be found on its downward slope—a hillside that falls down and away below your vantage point. This means that you look over the top of your potential garden site rather than onto it as with a level site, or up into it as with an upward slope. Such a condition makes for difficult gardening, but it offers the delight and exhilaration of the promontory experience, in which you can look way out upon the landscape, with a long view of the sky.

One way to use a downhill slope for gardening is to create a series of terraces that step down and away from the house. At the very least, you will need to carve out a flat area for viewing at the top of the slope as a level terrace for the house to sit on. Such a vantage point will feel precarious unless you create a strong turned-up edge or parapet wall at its outside perimeter; one that feels substantial enough to stop you from falling down the slope. Inside of this wall, you can create a viewing area with a terrace, pergola, reflecting pool, or planted border that acts as the close-up focal point. From such a high place, your focal point could also be a faraway scene — a mountain range, a distant lake, a village, or even a city off in the distance. Or perhaps, it is simply a view of nearby hills and trees. Placing vertical elements in the foreground, such as columns, piers, statues, or upright trees, you have many opportunities to create an interesting garden. You can terrace the slope and plant on each level, as many cultures do on steep terrain. You can use the slope as a backdrop for a collection of special plants — for example, a display of carefully clipped topiary trees or any of the solutions I mentioned for the upward slope.

One of my favorite slope experiences can be found at the garden of Shugaku-in Rikyu Imperial Villa in Kyoto. Here, you ascend a steep hillside to reach a viewing pavilion that sits on its summit. You follow a gravel and stone path that snakes upward through a planting of many species of shrubs that have been clipped together at a uniform height. You feel as if you're in a tunnel, unable to see over them until you've reached your goal. As you turn 180 degrees to face the view, you find yourself in front of a complete surprise: a pristine lake and island garden below with mountainscape beyond. The contrast between the tunnel-like experience in the shrubs and the long view out over them from the top is breathtaking.

Chapter 7

Enclosures

*Create enclosures that feel
like sheltering arms.*

VERY garden should feel like a refuge. A refuge
offers us a space of serenity in direct contrast to
the workaday world outside of its sheltering arms.
   Imagine leaning back into the soft depths of
an easy chair, one that seems to hold you in its
arms the way your parent did when you were a child. You feel
soothed, secure, and serene because you are surrounded by this harborlike enclosure on three sides. This is the feeling that enclosures —
walls, fences, hedges — can bring to you in your garden.
   You don't have to build high impenetrable walls or to create a
maze of impassable spaces to give yourself the feeling of enclosure
that you seek. All you may need is a corner that "backs you up" in
order to feel comfortable in contemplating your garden. If you are
lucky, a wall of tall trees, a forest, or grove that grew up between
you and your neighbors provides sufficient screening to block out
the outside world. Most of us are not so fortunate: We need to build

All you may need is a corner that "backs you up" in order to feel comfortable in contemplating your garden

an enclosure to set off our property as distinct. As we'll see, enclosures can be used to subdivide your property into a series of distinct
garden rooms, or define your space as a single unified whole.

WALLS

Constructed from elements of the earth, walls can be used as enclosures that follow the contours of your land or as architectural elements that take their cue from the design of the house. There are
many kinds of walls to consider using as delineators of your property.
A New England stone fence is the simplest of walls, placed as
a boundary marker with rocks pulled out of the stony earth when
tilling fields. A "hen's tooth" wall is created by setting a line of tall
standing stones that are buried up to their waists in earth, often used
as the simplest kind of retaining wall. A "ha-ha" wall also creates a
change in level: at its lower elevation, it acts as a visible retaining
element for walling in sheep and other livestock; at its upper elevation, it sits flush with the ground plane, allowing visitors to enjoy an
uninterrupted view onto the sheep field and the whole landscape
beyond.

"Freestanding walls" often show off the artistry of the mason:
Dry stone walls are carefully pieced stones set — like a jigsaw puzzle —
without mortar; variations of the same include mortar but with hidden joints; and some walls are beautifully pieced yet set in a bed of
mortar. Brick walls are often architectural in nature; they can be
stepped to follow a contour, topped with stone, rounded to create
corners, or laid in a serpentine pattern that curves in and out to
create planting pockets. Stucco is also a material of choice in many
parts of the country — it can be poured in place or constructed of
concrete blocks, stippled, painted, and made to look old. Mud brick or
adobe is a sculptural material used to create perimeter walls as well as
houses, gateways, benches, and curbs throughout the southwest.

Walls can be capped with stone or roofed with clay tiles; they can be built up or faced with a combination of materials; or topped with an openwork wood or wrought-iron fence so that a boundary is marked yet one can see through. An expensive part of any garden's design, a wall may be its most satisfying, for it is part landscape and part architecture, and, when well executed, a beautiful enclosure for any magic land.

FENCES

A well-designed fence also acts as an extension of your house into your landscape. Built of wood, iron, or bamboo, a good fence can pull the style, color, proportions, texture, and materials of a building into the garden. Few owners pay attention to the design of their fencing, and they are often surprised when their new and costly enclosure seems to detract from their house's charm. If you think of your fence as a piece of fine outdoor furniture, then you will take the time and necessary care to get the details right.

Consider some of the fences you've seen that somehow look all wrong. The six-foot stockade fence that surrounds the stately Victorian home, for instance, is a mixed metaphor combining images of dusty horse ranches with ornate San Francisco Painted Ladies. A better match for such a house might be a low openwork fence with turned spindles stained to match the body color or trim boards of the house. Sometimes a fence may be an appropriate choice to fit the architecture but is poorly installed. Imagine a simple white picket fence that matches the center-entrance colonial that it surrounds but is laid out so the top is tilted, rather than horizontal. When a formal fence "rakes"—slants so that it follows the groundplane—it can be visually jarring, perhaps because it needs to work as a piece of architecture rather than as an element of the natural landscape like a wall.

...work fences are symbolic and ornamental: They are not meant to keep people out so much as to visually ...e the garden area.

A better way of solving changes in level is to step a fence up or downhill in consistent increments.

A fence, to be stable, needs to turn a corner. Think of a run of fencing that fronts a house and stops at the driveway. It feels plunked down, and seems as though you could push it right over because it has no corner at either end to support it, both physically and psychologically. After all, a fence is an *enclosure*: It needs to enclose something and won't do its job if it doesn't provide a feeling of being inside of something that wraps around you, like a pair of sheltering arms.

There are two basic kinds of fences: openwork fences that allow the viewer to see over or through them, such as picket, spindle, and wrought-iron fences; and board fences that block views, such as stockade and shadow-box fences. Openwork fences are symbolic and ornamental: They are not meant to keep people out so much as to visually define the garden area, add architectural ornamentation that augments the design of the house, and to allow people to peep in. Board fences are meant to provide a visual barrier or to screen outside from inside. They are privacy fences designed to keep people and animals out (or in, as in the case of the family dog or toddler) and to allow little visual penetration onto the property. Sometimes, the two types can be combined into one, where the bottom two-thirds of a fence provides privacy, and the highest third is designed as an openwork, more ornamental "topper."

A rustic fence can provide an inexpensive alternative. In situations where the property line is far from the house, a grapestake or wire fence that blends in with surrounding vegetation might look just fine. Or if your property sits adjacent to a busy road, then employing a high rustic board fence to block views and sounds will inexpensively solve the problem of traffic lights and noise. Of course, different communities have different mandated fence heights and standards, so you need to check your town's building code before you select or install a fence.

HEDGES

A hedge is a fence made of living material. It may be left to grow in its natural state or pruned to look like an architectural element of the garden. You can create hedges of a single species or mixed plantings;

of trees or shrubs or both. You can prune hedges in all sorts of shapes, using sweeping curves or strict straight lines. I've seen hedges that look like crenellated castle walls, or dragon's backs, or pyramids; double hedges, hedges pruned as tunnels, and even clipped to create a little vegetative house.

One way of screening one property from another is to create a loose hedge of an array of trees. It seems that every job I've worked on recently has needed instant screening—the kind that you can only get with large trees. Such a hedge has the advantage of height: If you look down onto your neighbors, for instance, the only way you can hide their house from yours is to screen it with trees of sufficient size. Or if a large industrial building looms above you, a few choice tall trees will break up the massive facade and begin to obscure it from view. A collection of stately trees also allows your enclosure to become a garden in and of itself. Walking at the foot of a set of beautifully shaped conifer and deciduous trees is magical; you feel dwarfed by their towering forms and enclosed within their drooping boughs.

Tapestry hedges are used to create visual interest on the vertical plane. These are hedges that are made up of a mix of plants all pruned together as one. Shrubs or trees may be arranged in regular alternating patterns and carefully clipped—such as beech and yew or holly and hornbeam—or are less formally distributed with a wide mix of plant material and only lightly pruned once a year (or not at all). Think about combining different species of plants—such as holly, viburnum, azalea, rhododendron, barberry—which will offer a range of texture, bloom period, and color throughout the year. For plant lovers especially, the mixed hedge offers a way to grow a great variety of shrubs in a small area.

Chapter 8

The Planting Palette

*Consider your plants' growing
requirements and forms over time.*

ALWAYS love the moment when snow falls across
the garden—when all the grays and browns of
late winter are suddenly covered in a pure white
cloth, brightening the drabness and unifying its
elements and forms. This is the moment when I
can best assess how well the garden reads as a coherent design. I
love the way the granite ledge that edges our property to the north
looms over the oval pattern of the lawn; the way the curve of the
hedge mimics and extends both shapes; and I see where new trees
are needed to give more enclosure on the vertical plane. Blanketed
with snow, the structure of the garden works well; now it is time
to make the plantings just as successful. Seize this moment and
make notes for when spring finally comes and you can start to
select and install the plantings that your garden requires to make
it magical.

My imagination works best—especially in my own garden—when I have a simple canvas to ponder. If you don't have snow to abstract your garden for you, then try squinting your eyes so that the garden looks blurry. When you do this, you start to see your land as Monet saw the world: as a series of soft shapes of color and texture, as simplified linear patterns, as voids and solids. Your garden becomes a canvas that needs certain colors, textures, accents, sweeps, and brush strokes to pull it together, so it is a beautiful painting that you can walk right into and enjoy in each of its four dimensions.

Four dimensions? Yes, because you are composing the elements of its length, its height, and its depth, over *time*. Every plant that you put into the ground has a life span that figures prominently in your garden's composition. You make choices of plants that reflect your desire for consistency or for change over time. Let's look at your planting palette of trees, shrubs, ground covers, and vines and examine how you can use them in your garden.

EXERCISE: WHAT KIND OF GARDENER ARE YOU?

Are you a gardener who adores plants? Or one who loves form and structure—who looks first at the design and second at what plants should fill it? It helps to identify which type of gardener you are before you begin, but in the end you will need to wear both hats to create a great garden.

If you are making a garden in order to possess favorite plants, start a collection of a particular species, acquire new varieties, or harvest vegetables and fruits, then the form of your garden will seem less important than ensuring that you place each plant in its appropriate growing conditions. But you cannot place one plant adjacent to another without considering the elements of design. You have to ask yourself: What effect does aesthetic placement have with regard to the size, shape, and habit of each plant; its flower color, scale, and period of bloom, and its leaf size, color, size, and texture? There are more considerations: How many of each plant should I get? And how should I lay them out? Geometrically? In a curvy line? As an accent to a rock or at the foot of a certain tree? These kinds of questions soon lead you to even more: What is the image that I am trying to create here? What picture am I trying to paint in this space with this and other plants?

If, on the other hand, you have a particular configuration that you want to superimpose on your land but don't know which plants to choose for your garden plan, then pretty soon you become a plantsperson, out of necessity. If your garden lies on a dry slope facing west, then whatever design you come up with will not work unless you can get the plants to grow well under the conditions that you have to work with. Soon you start looking in catalogs and reference books for plants that can tolerate dry, hot slopes, and you realize that your design will prosper by using only these plants (unless you are able to drastically change the conditions by irrigating, by creating a canopy overhead, or by bulldozing the slope to make it take another form). You cannot carry out the design of your dreams unless the plants will be happy in the conditions that are provided for them; you need to learn as much as you can about plants.

The two approaches are symbiotic: They each need something of the other in order to make a lovely and coherent whole. Be a designer as you plant and a plantsperson as you design, and your garden will thrive in its form as well as in its details.

TREES: VERTICAL ELEMENTS

Trees provide a filigreed screen between the garden and its surrounding environment. The tallest trees—like oaks, maples, and beeches—rise sixty feet or more on one trunk like umbrellas above the garden, with leafy boughs set high between ground and sky. Their foliage shades the garden from the heat of the summer sun, while in winter their structure is revealed, acting as a filter for winter winds and light. Tall evergreen trees such as pines or spruces create a different effect: They grow up out of the ground like feathery plumes, their branches start low and spire upward, and their needles softly veil the view beyond. As the backbone plantings of your garden, such tall trees need to be carefully selected and appropriately placed, for they are the least moveable members of your planting palette. Their shade, roots, and height will also determine the scale and the conditions of the plantings around them. Consult reference books, horticulturists, and nurseries before deciding on a tree; understand how much space it occupies at maturity in all its three dimensions—its height and breadth above the ground, and its depth and root structure below the ground.

The Planting Palette

• • • • • •

Domestic gardens tend to be planted with smaller ornamental trees that fit nicely under or up against the largest trees that may be already present on your land.

Domestic gardens tend to be planted with smaller ornamental trees that fit nicely under or up against the largest trees that may be already present on your land. These twenty to thirty-foot trees create canopy and enclosure but at a scale that suits a small property. The range of forms of such ornamentals is wonderful: vase-shaped (some crabapples), fan-shaped (autumn cherries), horizontally branched (dogwoods, Japanese maples), oval (Bradford pears), broad (magnolia) or narrow (birches), weeping (Sargent's weeping hemlock), or spires (cedars), to mention only a few. The best small trees should provide several seasons of interest. Some flower in the spring or in the early summer (magnolia, mountain ash); others enjoy brilliant autumn color (amelanchier); still others grow showy berries (hawthorn), and others display fascinating bark patterns on their trunks (stewartia).

The problem is how to arrange them. As always, you must make some choices: First, do you want to create a forest or an orchard; a glade or a dell; a hedge or a specimen planting? Do you want unity—the same species of trees—or variety—a mixture of different species? Matching these images to the conditions of your yard—the amount of sun and shade, the prevailing winds, and the soils, will all start to help you decide what to buy and where to place it. One garden I designed was a north-facing urban garden surrounded by four-story buildings with a huge linden tree overhead. I asked myself, "What small ornamental trees could I plant in such difficult and dark conditions?" After researching possible candidates, I felt that I had only one choice: Japanese maples that could tolerate poor growing conditions and would provide a beautiful horizontal structure throughout the year, a leafy canopy in summer, and brilliant leaf color in autumn. Now some five years after planting, the three green maples have survived their ordeal and continue to give this little city garden the natural superstructure that it needs.

EXERCISE: PUTTING PLANTS TOGETHER AS VIGNETTES

Since I am a visual person, I like to select my materials in person at a nursery. There is nothing more fun than visiting a good-sized nursery with a wide selection, helpful staff, and your own well-developed imagination, and choosing the very plants that will make it into your garden. Each visit can be a learning experience: You develop your visual range and practical knowledge, your planting palette, and your appreciation for the many horticultural treasures available on the market. I recommend that you go on your own or with a trustworthy and knowledgeable individual (landscape designer, contractor, or gardening friend) and just walk around, taking notes on what you like and exclaiming over what you must have. Tag those plants immediately and note their height, breadth, their ultimate growth, and habit. Make a list of secondary material that might be good for background plantings or for filler shrubs. Then go home and figure out how to make them work in situ.

This system works well because you know the plants that are coming—they feel like old friends—and you have spent time planning where best to place them. When you actually get them all in one place, you will undoubtedly change your plans, but usually for the better. If you use your visual sense well, designing your plantings will give you the same enjoyment as doing a jigsaw puzzle—

when the last piece of the puzzle goes into place, you have a marvelous sense of well-being and your garden looks wonderful.

If you squint your eyes and imagine your land populated with the umbrella-like height and breadth of tall deciduous shade trees, underplanted with the plumes of conifers and the varied shapes of smaller ornamental trees, you will begin to understand the sizes, forms, and characteristics of the trees that you might choose for your garden. Once you know that you would like to plant an evergreen corner of your property, under a huge existing oak, softened in the foreground with spring-flowering woodsy-looking small ornamentals that would flank a stone bench, then you can select your species: how about cryptomeria or Alaskan cedar for the evergreens, and autumn cherry or kousa dogwood for the smaller deciduous trees? After making a list of possibilities that will thrive in the conditions at hand, will grow to an acceptable height and width, and will flower when you would like to see color in that area, then you can choose your candidate, buy and install it, knowing you have made an excellent choice that suits your vision, the requirements of the plant, and the conditions of the land.

SHRUBS: TRANSITIONAL ELEMENTS

Shrubs create middle-story enclosures in our gardens. They bridge the gap between the vertical elements and the ground plane and carve out space into separate identifiable areas. Shrubs create a body of land in the garden, defining its spaces, edging paths, creating harbors or promontories, and softening rocks or sculptures. Masses of shrubs that have grown together feel like a miniature landscape of hills and dales or a "shoreline" that rises above the lawn like an embankment. Planted as drifts of one species such as rhododendron, as a mixed grouping of broadleaf shrubs, or interplanted with perennials, grasses, and bulbs, these borders are the backbone and transitional plane that knits together the whole garden.

Most books tell you to learn about how big a shrub will become and plant it accordingly, leaving plenty of space between specimens so that they have room to grow. This leaves your garden with gaps between plantings for many years, which you can choose to plug with ground covers while you wait. In Japan we learned a different way: We planted shrubs so that their branches would just touch, allowing them to grow up together as a mass, while pruning them at least once a year to keep them in check. We would plant many colors of flowering azaleas together, not in large drifts, but as spots of color, their different hues tempered by their foliage. We would intermix early, mid, and late-blooming azaleas with billows of spiraea, spiky mountain andromeda, and dark-green junipers to give the feeling of a vast mountainscape in miniature. High shrubs can also be pruned together to create enclosures: I have seen a mix of enkianthus—a tall deciduous bush with lily-of-the-valley like panicles that bloom in May—with forsythia, shrubby dogwoods, quince, and even shrub roses.

It is increasingly important to me to use evergreen shrubs in quantity to get my clients through the six months of leafless weather that we experience in the Northeast. Since I can count on two hands the genuses of broadleaf shrubs for shade that can tolerate our climate, I need to become ever-creative about how to use them. In one recent project, we combined masses of a single broadleaf species such as inkberry with drifts of tall grasses, red-twigged dogwood, and early-blooming bulbs to create interest throughout the year. When you begin to creatively combine the many different types of plants in service of a particular design goal, the artistic potential is vast.

GROUND COVERS AND VINES: THE HORIZONTAL AND VERTICAL CARPETS

If you did nothing else but plant ground covers and vines in your garden last year, you probably feel satisfied with your work today. Ground covers—low plants that cover the bare dirt—are numerous and varied: Grass, bulbs, perennials, ornamental grasses, and mosses can all be used to carpet your garden in elegant and satisfying ways. Trees define the vertical zone in a garden; shrubs the middleground zone; and ground covers the horizontal or ground level. As I discussed previously in the section of chapter 3 called "Meadows," there are many ways to think about planting your garden carpet to bring unity to your garden.

I like to think of a meadow as a kind of carpet on the floor of a landscape; similarly, a lawn is a kind of carpet on the floor of a garden. As in a room, this carpet can be a soft, uniform background or a varied, visual field with a pattern all of its own. Such a pattern can be formal—as in a knot garden or parterre planting, or informal—as in a lawn naturalized with daffodils; or a cottage garden planted in a wild mixture of perennials, annuals, and vegetables.

The most enchanting garden carpet I have ever seen is at Winterthur, the 900-acre Delaware estate that was home to Henry Francis du Pont from his birth in 1880 until his death in 1969, now open to the public. In the wonderful Azalea Woods, a high canopy of oaks, hickories, maples, beech, and tulip-poplars grew tall above

ike to think of a meadow as a kind of carpet on the floor of a landscape; similarly, a lawn is a kind of rpet on the floor of a garden.

an understory of dogwood trees that proliferate at the woodland's edge, below which kurume hybrid azaleas drift in clouds of pastel colors. Underfoot, thousands upon thousands of bulbs and perennials bloom from late winter into the autumn. No matter when you go, waves of ground covers delight: From the earliest drifts of snowdrops, a continually changing display of naturalized cochicums, anemones, Spanish, Virginia, and English bluebells, woodland phlox, buttercups, mayapples, trillium, hepatica, and Italian windflower, all blossom in Mr. du Pont's enchanted forest.

Vines create a carpet on the vertical plane. Walls, fences, and buildings that are drenched in climbing plants blur the usual distinction between architectural and landscape elements, eroding edges and softening angles with light-reflecting leaves and bright blossoms. Boston's venerable Beacon Hill boasts narrow streets faced by old brick townhouses that enjoy postage stamp-sized back gardens. Every year in mid-May, one can visit many of these "Secret Gardens of Beacon Hill" to see how different owners handle their tiny shady spaces. One gasps at the level changes, the fountains, the ironwork, the statues, and the plantings, but what always delights the most are the three-story brick walls that are literally blanketed in vines: Boston and English ivy, climbing hydrangea, and sometimes, with the right exposure, wisteria. When the crowds clear, you feel as though you stand deep within a leafy chapel, lost in verdant thoughts.

When they were young, my daughters' favorite bedtime reading was a little book called *Flower Fairies of the Garden*, by Cicely Mary Barker. Different flowers were given names and personalities: the Heliotrope Fairy, the Lilac Fairy, the Rose Fairy, and so on, each described in poetry and depicted in delightful drawings. We'd pore through the book to find which fairy most resembled which daughter. This lovely little book made flowers magical for my girls, just as real flowers make gardens so enchanting for us all.

The Planting Palette

• • • • • •

Flowers delight the senses. We revel in their fragrance, their hues, their graceful forms. Whether a flowering tree, shrub, vine, perennial, annual, or bulb, a flower also performs a function: It is the reproductive portion of any plant that is an angiosperm, the largest group of modern plants. We revel in a field of black-eyed Susans or in a peony border, in a stand of flowering cherries or a banking of heathers in bloom. To design our gardens around flowers, we must learn the many characteristics of each: when it blooms and for how long, how tall and wide it becomes, and its soil requirements and maintenance needs. The artistry comes in creating combinations of plants—in making outdoor flower arrangements in your garden that work as well as cut flowers arranged in a vase. How does one begin?

You could make a garden around a single color scheme: a white garden, a yellow garden, a blue garden; or a garden around a single plant species: a lavender field, a shrub rose *allée*, a Michaelmas daisy (aster) garden, as English plantswoman Gertrude Jekyll did. Poet John Donne wrote verse about an "alphabet of flowers"—another idea for a garden. You can make a woodland garden, an herb terrace, or a mixed border; each requires specific knowledge about selected plants. To be a good flower arranger in your garden, though, you need to move plants around until they feel right.

Claude Monet learned about horticulture by planning, planting, and then rearranging his garden at Giverny. He mixed a flower palette of irises, orchids, wisteria, narcissus, roses, hollyhocks, nasturtiums, and a host of other favorites in his borders, on archways, and as bankings in his two-and-a-half acre space. Like an extended cottage garden, the flower borders are voluptuous with blossoms of impressionistic hues. In speaking of his garden, Monet once said, "I am enraptured"—and so are we.

Chapter 9

Patterns on the Earth

Gardens can be organized in formal or informal patterns.

ARDENS are really cleaned up, organized versions of nature. How you interpret "nature" will determine the form of your garden. Does your sense of nature suggest patterns that are formal or informal? Geometric or curvilinear? Symmetrical or asymmetrical? Architectural or free-form?

At one end of the spectrum is the Pool Garden at Bloedel Reserve on Bainbridge Island, Washington. This is an architectural space surrounded by high evergreen trees and a lower, perfectly pruned yew hedge, dominated by an oblong reflecting pool. Cut out of the forest, the space shocks and delights; someone's strong sense of order demanded a geometric garden room where a conifer forest had once stood.

In contrast, the Moss Garden at Bloedel Reserve is a landscape that looks untamed but is just tweaked a bit to make it less scruffy and more beautiful. This verdant garden looks completely natural, with the trunks and roots of trees encrusted with moss and the limbs cleaned up so that more light and air can enter the velvet space. A simple gravel path winds its way through the area, leading to the Pool Garden through a landscape so naturalistic that it nearly doesn't seem to be a garden at all.

The Pool Garden's perfect symmetry and the formality of its design was probably inspired by Western gardening patterns; the Moss Garden's naturalness was probably inspired by oriental antecedents. As far as anyone knows, the two gardening traditions started quite independently of each other in two very different lands: Egypt and China. These ancient cultures developed diametrically opposed horticultural styles with which to shape the land, based on their societies and the landscape they inhabited: formal patterns and informal patterns.

FORMAL PATTERNS

The Egyptian garden grew out of the need for enclosed, irrigated land in the desert. Its formal language—drawn from a rigid cultural tradition that didn't substantially change for thousands of years—was transmitted first to the Greeks and Romans, then to the Persians, the Mughals, the Italians, and the French. While each culture varied the forms somewhat, certain principles were common to each: the organization of a garden around an axis on both sides of which parts are arranged in a symmetrical way; and the use of straight lines throughout. In Egyptian and Persian gardens, the quadripartite plan was the design of choice. It was based on the form of a cross and said to represent the four quarters of the universe. Italian gardens were highly architectural, created with masonry staircases, pavilions, cascades, and avenues, all of which were softened by the beauty of the surrounding hillsides and the elaborate use of water throughout the garden in the form of pools, water stairs, and ornamental patterns using spray jets. The formal tradition reached its apex when the French garden designer Le Nôtre enlarged its scale at Versailles, the palace of Louis XIV. Le Nôtre created magnificent parterres, canals, avenues, and *allées* that covered 250 acres, taking the idea of an axial plan to its limit. Oriented around a grand axis, Versailles also includes cross-axes at right angles, diagonals, and circles that offered clearings in the forested space.

In today's garden, a formal layout offers simple solutions for conceiving of, designing, and setting out a garden. Formal gardens satisfy the eye because they are understandable in one glance as a whole. They require perfect placement and patterning: Every object must be set symmetrically—exactly opposite to its mate. The smallest deviation feels just slightly off kilter and ruins the effect. People love formal gardens for their patterns: Intricate parterres, shell motifs, heraldic emblems, knot gardens, and reflecting pools create a kind of oriental carpet on the ground plane. *Allées*, swags, tunnels, and central foci like obelisks and fountains can keep the viewer oriented on the vertical plane. Some of the most beautiful gardens in the world are based on symmetrical principles of design: as discussed, France's Versailles, Great Britain's Sissinghurst, Italy's Villa Medici, Kashmir's Shalimar Gardens, and Washington's Dumbarton Oaks. These gardens are designed using different geometric shapes that offer their visitors a wide range of different feelings. The following section looks at the effect some of these patterns have on the design of gardens.

Squares and Rectangles

A square design can be accused of becoming boring. No matter where you look, you understand its layout immediately, especially when all four corners are treated in the same way. Yet its very predictability is also the delight of the square design: It is in the details that the plan can come alive. You can change the pattern from one side to another; change the plants or their color, shape, and textures; or alter the benches in each corner. Suddenly, the square that seemed so dogmatic before begins to break down, it becomes a strong structure against which something surprising can take place.

There is nothing wrong with perfection however. Squares work beautifully with the geometry of a house, built up as it is on planes, and orthogonal and plumb lines. If applied to the open space in front of a house, a square is most effective when designed as a flat plane to be used as an entry court, a terrace, or an activity space for games and social interaction. A square can be used to dramatic effect when it becomes a surprise planted off in the wilderness far removed from the house. Its strength lies in its relationship to the house or its complete lack of such; in its surprising and sudden taming of nature in some out-of-the-way place.

Herb gardens, chessboard gardens, and cloisters are all planted with square layouts. They can be filled with grass, pools or fountains, parterre plantings, meadows, terraces, and sculptures.

Rectangles are anchored squares: They have two ends that seem like perfect harbors for positioning oneself within to survey the rest of the garden scene. If you lay out a rectangle parallel to the house the effect is quite different from locating it on the perpendicular: The former upholds the geometry of the house, and the latter becomes an axial pattern, offering the possibility of ending the rectangle with a focal point—a balustrade for viewing out, a gazebo, or a statue. The plane of the rectangle may be sunken, raised, moated, walled, paved, or patterned.

Circles

A circle may be the most meditative pattern on earth. Like the sacred syllable "om," considered to be the greatest of all the mantras, a circle is open, continuous, and omni-directional. It seems to emanate from

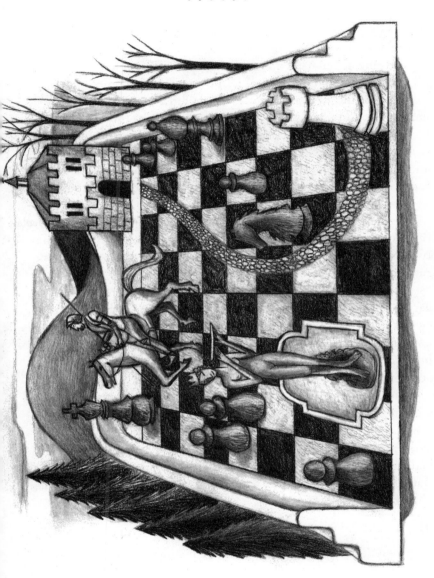

Herb gardens, chessboard gardens, and cloisters are all planted with square layouts.

the void space at its very center, upon which you can focus and extend your mind. As when a raindrop falls upon a still pool, sending out rings from its center to the pond's edge, so too a circle can fill a garden with its presence. In a Japanese meditation garden, a focal tree trunk emerging from a field of gravel raked in a circular pattern around it seems to fill the silence with its intensity. A perfectly round yew-hedged garden room astonishes the mind. A millstone offers the perfect threshold—a pausing place for both mind and body. In your garden, you can create circular patterns in the form of a *point rond*, ring, rondelle, fairy circle, crown, diadem, coronet, garland, ring, or necklace.

If you place benches opposite one another at the edge of a circle, the form will feel like an ellipse—a weighted circle. An ellipse has two clear pausing places—two harbors that orient the design as a rectangle with a semicircle at each end.

Circles can be planted in quadrants and opened with paths at each of four openings. Bisecting paths can often act like decorative elements themselves; and placing one down the middle of a circle is another way to orient you in space. Plantings can guide you by being different or can keep you moving round and round by being constantly the same.

Circles can be filled with gravel, grass, plantings, terraces; within them you can place pools and ponds, fountains, statues, a singular cosmic tree, pergola or arbor, or any combination of the above. Because of their strong geometry, they often look best walled, hedged, edged with boxwood or perennials, or accented with small statues. A circular lawn can focus attention away from rectangular boundaries.

Triangles

A garden designed in the shape of an equilateral triangle feels balanced and restful. Its form allows you to choose one of three different corners for sitting, each with a view out onto a different scene. An isosceles triangle is more directional: It looks like an arrowhead that points a certain way. Because its legs are formed by strong diagonals, the triangle's insistent directionality makes a strong statement on the landscape. If you place a number of triangles together, you can begin to form other shapes: the chevron—a heraldic symbol consisting of two diagonal stripes meeting at a point; and the *étoile*—a star-shaped pattern formed by five or more triangles whose short sides form a pentagon in the middle. Leo Tolstoy's *étoile* was formed around a huge old beech tree with gravel paths surrounded by Russian wildflowers—a formal design executed with native materials. You can also use triangles to create octagons with alternating beds of different-colored annuals or perennials, vegetables, or gravel.

Knot gardens can be designed by combining circles and squares, triangles, and rectangles, and highlighting the resulting patterns with plantings and ground covers. More and more I enjoy using these geometric shapes in unusual ways: plunking a perfect square of grass into a perfect circle of black river stones in a small urban back garden, or using a propeller form whose shape seems to spin the visitor in and out of a basic circle plan to relate to an existing sculpture that spirals up into the air.

My favorite use of an abstract but regular shape was a maze design taken from a sketch showing some of the dance movements for the minuet, a slow, graceful dance performed in the eighteenth century in three-four time. I took the pattern that showed how two people would spiral in from opposite directions to meet at the center, and created a garden out of it. You can also use patterns from all over the world as your starting point: Celtic symbols, Native American drawings, quilt patterns, musical inscriptions, poetic meters—all suggest beautiful patterns that might help you create a magic land that draws from your own background or interests.

INFORMAL PATTERNS

Different than the Western tradition that began by trying to reclaim small pieces of a vast desert, the Eastern tradition began with enclosing the natural landscape itself. In China, the earliest gardens were large hunting parks for the emperors, ordered by architectural elements, including buildings, gateways, terraces, and steps, and always enclosed. These, and the later private gardens built by scholars and merchants, were both based on the principle of creating a harmonious relationship between humans and nature; in the East, gardens were meant for contemplation of the landscape, and were based upon philosophical and poetic myths and precepts. Landscape painting and gardening advanced in tandem, reaching their highest level in China during the Sung dynasty.

The Japanese, influenced by Chinese culture through envoys sent around A.D. 700, developed their own version of abstracted nature in their gardens. Their tradition of *karesansui* — "dry water mountain" gardens — were created as aids to enlightenment for Zen Buddhist monks. These abstracted islands, mountains, and miniature landscapes set in a "sea" of gravel were artistic attempts to reduce and distill the natural landscape to its very essence.

There is no clear evidence that the English landscape tradition evolved in response to the influence of oriental gardening ideals, yet similarities exist: Each created allegorical journeys through a cleaned-up version of a natural landscape. In eighteenth-century England, however, strong classical overtones guided the placement of the sweeping lawns, lakes, belts of trees, and many architectural features — all set along circuit walks, often miles long.

More and more, our Western contemporary gardens are based on Eastern principles of informality, asymmetry, and naturalness. Giving up a geometric layout is not always easy. You need to substitute a clear image in order to create something informal. Look back to chapter 3, "Enchanted Landscapes," for some of these images: a dell, glade, forest, rockery, or wilderness are all useful forms that you might use for your garden.

I try several different approaches to help get started in designing an informal garden: abstracting the landscape; going with the flow; and going native. Let's look at each one.

Abstracting the Landscape

When you abstract a landscape, you strip it down to its essentials and choose certain elements to stand out as important. You can create an abstracted landscape in your own garden in one of three ways: make what exists more pristine, import a new landform or landscape as a focus, or recreate a landscape in miniature.

When you have a beautiful piece of land, sometimes the most appropriate thing to do with it is simply clean it up — to abstract it by making it pure. The easiest method is to remove all dead limbs and undergrowth. This allows you to see each undulation on the groundplane, to enjoy each stone that may have tumbled there, and to appreciate existing trees as individuals or as groupings. Encouraging the growth of existing ground covers or importing new ones can help you emphasize the beauty of the land; carefully pruning your trees to rid them of deadwood or diseased branches, to limb them up off the ground, or to open their canopy up to light and air, allows you to honor what exists as beautiful and to make it the backbone of your garden. Once you have made your land pristine, you can choose locations for paths, benches, and new plantings that will make the garden more complete. Don't neaten it up everywhere, though — keep a few dead trees and scruffy areas to attract birds.

Another way of abstracting the landscape is to create a completely new landform or landscape, one that wasn't present before. Creating a pond in a low spot or building a rocky stream across your lawn focuses your garden around a new element — an abstracted piece of the landscape imported into your backyard. When you do this, of course, you create a whole scale change. A friend who lives on a busy street had a flat site surrounded by a fence. Bothered by the incessant traffic noise and headlights, she decided to block it all out for good by creating a long and high berm on the roadside, an abstracted arm of land that has brought privacy and peace to her back garden area.

You can also abstract the landscape by capturing it in miniature. This is what Zen masters tried to do in creating meditation gardens. One triangular rock can stand for a whole mountain; a small-leafed azalea suggests a verdant hillock; white-raked gravel becomes a shiny sea. I have created small entry landscapes of moss and stone, moon-viewing "pools" of ivy, and sandy shorelines edged with bearberry and sedges that imitate beachfront along the Atlantic shore. Japanese designers also imported entire scenes from famous and beloved places and recreated them in miniature in their gardens. What were considered the "three most beautiful landscapes" were copied throughout Japan: the islands of Matsushima; the Itsukushima-jinja shrine; and the Amanohashidate, the "bridge of heaven"—a spit of land in the Bay of Miyazu to the northwest of Japan. This last landscape was replicated time after time, with the most famous characterization at Katsura Imperial Palace in Kyoto, a country villa of the princes of the Imperial family. At the tip of a pebbled promontory sits a rough-hewn stone lantern, a miniature version of Amanohashidate shrunken to fit the size dictated by these residential palace grounds. It's fun to think about what American "beautiful landscapes" one could abstract and recreate in a garden: how about the Grand Canyon in Arizona, the Old Man in the Mountain in New Hampshire, or the redwood forests of California?

Going with the Flow

Another way of creating an informal layout for your garden is to think of it all as part of a stream that flows from one part of the garden to the next. For example, look out at your existing lawn. Now scrunch up your eyes and imagine that it is a pool of space that "floods" the floor of your garden landscape. Imagine that the grassy areas are filled with water—that whatever used to be ground cover is now liquid. How does this liquid flow through the garden? Using water as a metaphor helps you see the groundplane of your garden as a series of connected areas—places where both water and people can flow through space; where a path is like a river and a place is like a pond. The idea of water also helps you imagine how the "banks" of your grassy "pond" should be formed: where they should be rounded—perhaps around a natural rock outcropping or near a grove of trees; and where they should be straight—such as near the house or the driveway. As in nature, the pond's edge needs to be raised, bermed, or constructed in such a way that erosion can't occur: using cobbles or bricks as a kind of dike, or planting soft billows of perennials that form a colorful shoreline, or placing stones and iris so that it feels like a rocky coast. Going with the flow of water is a powerful metaphor that helps you know how and where to place many of the elements in your garden, so they work together as a cohesive idea that makes inherent sense both to you and to your garden visitor.

I think of my paths as being like a riverscape flowing across my land. The road outside the garden walls is like a big river, off of which my entry path is like a meandering stream. Where I want a broad path for strolling side-by-side, I pretend that the walkway is an open brook that is shallow and moves slowly but directly downstream. Where I want my visitors to walk single file with their eyes at their feet, I construct a rivulet that twists and turns, carving out deep shores in some spots, and beaches in others. Where I want people to gather, I construct a terrace, which I imagine as a pond that feels contained and complete. Where I want people to descend a staircase, I imagine it as a waterfall that is narrow and rushing at the apex, but widens into a pool at its base. After all, a path is like

The Magic Land

· · · · · ·

Look out at your existing lawn. Now scrunch up your eyes and imagine that it is a pool of space that "floods" the floor of your garden landscape.

water—a force of nature through which people ebb, flow, trickle, stream, flood, whirl, glide, spill, or cascade. As Pascal said, a stream is a "moving road." As you design your garden layout and make adjustments to what you already have created, thinking about "going with the flow" offers you an elegant image for creating a garden that feels like a part of nature.

Another kind of stream that you can incorporate into the layout of your garden is the *ch'i* or "cosmic breath" that runs through your site. *Feng shui* is the ancient Chinese version of geomancy—a specialized art by which propitious locations are selected. Masters of this art believed that currents running through the earth could influence events and the fortunes of people. Therefore, diviners would help believers site buildings and graves according to the relation between winds (*feng*), water (*shui*), and the hills and valleys of the landscape in which they lived. Certain orientations were auspicious and others were considered taboo. Most beneficial was to place your house so that it faced south, was located two-thirds of the way up a slope on dry ground, enjoyed the protection of lower hills to the east and west, and had a reservoir or pool of water directly below the house. Since evil spirits were thought to travel in straight lines, it was important to create entrances that were off-axis from one another, and to create winding paths and curvilinear walls within a residence. Gardens were always surrounded by walls to create a peaceful enclosure that would hold good influences within them. Today, the practice of *feng shui* has gained popularity, with many books available on the subject and consultants ready to analyze the exterior and interior layout of one's house or apartment. Understanding the flow of forces on your site may help you to know how best to lay out the elements upon it.

Going Wild

In chapter 3, "Enchanted Landscapes," I discussed the concept of "wild gardens," which were popular in the nineteenth century and planted with indigenous species found in the wild. You can also create an informal garden based on this ecologically sensitive model; consider your region's landscape and its cultural heritage as you plan your design. Looking closely at the surrounding materials, land-scapes, and structures to suggest the layout of your garden—rather than to Italian, French, English, or Japanese ideals—can help you begin to "see" the design on your land. Because of our diverse set of cultures and geographic conditions, there is really no such thing as an "American" garden typology. Instead, each region offers different possibilities for creating new garden forms, that reflect its particular people and surroundings. Regional garden designs include Illinois prairie meadows, New Mexican cactus gardens, Colorado Rocky Mountain high-slope xeriscapes, New England rockeries, Virginia azalea gardens, and California coastal-scrub borders. Look to your region to go wild with your garden's design.

Another kind of wild garden that has merit for our modern land-scapes is the so-called cottage garden, an English vernacular style that consists of a seemingly casual mixture of vegetables, flowering plants, fruit trees, and shrubs. What might seem like the random nature of many cottage gardens—designed as a potpourri of beloved plants, rather than a strictly formal arrangement—may seem chaotic but is usually organized according to deep love and knowledge of each plant. Perhaps the most informal of possible garden layouts, the cottage garden is not for everyone; just for those who delight in serendipity, spontaneity, and a certain level of delightful chaos.

Chapter 10

Composing the Journey

Compose physical and mental journeys through your garden.

HEN you strip a garden to its essentials, it is really made up of only two elements: paths and places. A *path* is designed for physical motion; a *place* is designed for quiescence—for being at rest. As we've seen, a place is really a vantage point, like a harbor, a promontory, or a cave; a path is the thread that binds one vantage to another. Each element can be thought of as being like a journey in time and in space: When one walks a path, one makes a voyage with one's feet—a physical journey; when one pauses in a place, one makes a mental voyage—a mind journey.

THE PHYSICAL JOURNEY

What are the elements of a physical journey? There are simply four: a departure point, a destination point, the events along the way, and a route that takes one from departure to destination and vice versa. These same elements are part of the garden journey that you make as well. If you can think clearly about each of these points, you will be able to better choreograph your garden's design.

Departure Point

First think about the departure point. When and where do you begin the experience of your garden? In the front yard you might walk through a hedge, a rose-clad arbor, or a swinging gate. Or you might stroll along the driveway to get to a brick path to the front door. If your garden lies at the back of the house, how do you get there? It is important to mark the entry to your garden and the point from which you have started to make a physical journey around it.

All gardens need a clear-cut departure point. This is often a gateway, opening, threshold, or structure that signals that the garden is open to one's strolling and viewing pleasure. It may be a set of French doors that open off the garden room of your house, or a deck from which you can see the garden before entering it. It may be a rustic gate made up of logs and twine that you walk under at the entrance to a woodland garden. It may be the dock to which you tether your rowboat, as you alight at your island cottage off the coast of Maine. A garden may have just one departure point or a series of them—each different garden room or collection of plants enjoying its own different gateway, sign, or threshold underfoot.

A departure point is usually suggested by a gateway overhead or a threshold underfoot, or both. Gateways are vertical markers that stand out in a landscape—urns that rise above the balustrade; twin cypress trees that announce the entrance to the adjacent formal garden; an ornate wrought-iron gazebo that stands at the intersection of four paths. Thresholds are the welcome mats of a garden: horizontal markers that carve out space in a landscape; for example, one large millstone that forms the intersection of several stepping-stone paths; a cobbled court from which you descend to the garden on stone steps; the semicircle of lawn from which you are meant to gaze over adjacent fields of grazing cows.

Destination Point

A destination point is different from a departure point. It is the place one longs to get to: the goal of the physical journey. The little huts of a garden—the pergolas, arbors, summerhouses, and gazebos—are all destination points along a garden path. Often a destination point enjoys a high vantage so you can look out and over where you were and where you intend to go—a place to contemplate the garden world. A destination point can be as unadorned as a park bench set along a gravel path or as elaborate as a stone grotto tucked into a fern-filled hillside. A common feature of each destination point is that in the same way that it may become a pausing place for your physical journey, it may also act as the departure point for your "mind journey."

Events

A journey would not be interesting without something happening along the way—the activities, landmarks, or points of interest that you enjoy while moving through space. For example, icebergs spied outside your porthole are an event on an ocean voyage. Your first sighting of land after five days at sea would be another event. Activities that happen on shipboard—a masquerade ball, a spectacular sunset, winning at bingo—are events that you might recount in your stories of your journey across the seas. Similarly, such events happen in a garden journey: You enter through a formal boxwood garden;

The Magic Land

• • • • •

A destination point . . . is the place one longs to get to: the goal of the physical journey.

pass under a bower of sweet-smelling clematis; spy a gnome poking his head out of a carpet of English ivy; come upon a little reflecting pool over which a silver pear tree weeps. These events are the special points of interest that you design for your visitor to enjoy and may be singular objects or even small gardens in themselves. Choosing a plethora of personally meaningful events is one way for your garden to take form.

Route

I find that the design of the garden route is the most magical part of creating the journey. Here, you have the most control over how your visitor perceives and enjoys your garden. The ribbon that unites one place to another, the path, may be carefully choreographed to enhance and alter your mood as you stroll.

Think about the difference between a wide path and a skinny one. A wide path allows you and another person to walk side by side, and it feels like a broad avenue through the garden. Such a path is useful in getting to the front door. In comparison, a narrow path is meant for walking single file and feels more naturally in tune with the land, like a squirrel trail trodden through a forest. The broad path is easy to maneuver—you can raise your head and look around you, whereas the narrow trail requires concentration so you don't "step off the path."

A straight path affects you differently from a meandering path. The first is goal-oriented, allowing you to move quickly toward your destination. The more circuitous path offers a lazier stroll. Its twists and turns, comings and goings, invite exploration; it is a mystery and a thrill to discover what lies just beyond the next bend. Such a path reveals itself slowly over time.

Topography can also be used to enhance the design of your garden's pathways. Ascending a mountain is a very different experience from descending it, even when using the same path in both directions. Going up, you tend to traverse—move sideways while climbing—and always look at your feet. You can stop and gaze to where the path becomes wide enough so you can turn around; but otherwise, the climb seems interminable and enervating. Throughout it all, you are eager and determined to reach your destination—the summit. Once there, you enjoy the fruits of your labors: a magnificent view.

When you go down the mountain, the reverse experience holds true: You have successfully reached your goal, and you feel light-hearted and free. You trip downhill, barely stopping to look at the scenery, your eyes still on your feet so you don't fall; your mind full of the events that you have just enjoyed. Using the contrast between the up and down experience suggests ways to make a pathway feel magical on a hilly site. You could create a long, meandering trail, for instance, that enjoys frequent rest stops as it ascends to the high point but then descends in a quick and efficient way. Or you could reverse the experience by making an arduous but direct stairway to the top and a leisurely way down along a different route.

With even the slightest change in grade, you can create the feeling of having climbed a great slope by the way that you choreograph the path. Leo Tolstoy's garden in Moscow, for example, was a flat two-acre site before he built a mound for contemplation. A snaky trail winds up this twelve-foot-high hillock to reach a simple wooden bench at the summit: a place for him to sit high and removed from his large and rambunctious family. Like Tolstoy's, your ability to direct your visitor's footsteps and influence his or her frame of mind while enjoying your garden is an important part of the art of garden design.

DESIGNING WITH STEPPING-STONES

I love to design journeys using stepping-stones because they are easy to maneuver and quickly expressive of the designer's intent.

Imagine that you have a pile of stepping-stones to select from in a range of sizes and shapes, but each is bearing a flat top and measures several inches thick. The object of this exercise is to get from your driveway to a side door in an efficient but interesting way. How do you begin to set out the stones?

First, I think about *thresholds:* pausing places between two points—inside and outside, up and down, sidewalk and garden, for example. Two places need thresholds on this little journey: the area immediately adjacent to the driveway and the point of entry into the house. I always make my thresholds of larger and longer stones: places where a visitor can place two feet, look up, and notice where the path leads; in other words, departure and destination points. I always set these stones first.

Then I set out the *moving stones:* the stones that are just big enough for one foot. I place stones in a meandering line in an alternating right-left-right-left gait pattern. If the path is particularly long, I like to break it up with another threshold stone so that the pace seems more easygoing than relentless. Sometimes, the path system becomes more complex: Perhaps a secondary path veers off from the main path to another part of the garden, so I would place a large, roundish threshold stone as a decision point for choosing one path over another. Or perhaps an "event" happens along the path—a bench or a statue, for example. In either case, I would create a little terrace-threshold to set it apart as special.

How high off the ground you set your stepping-stones, how large they are, how far apart from each other they sit, and how they meander through space are all important design considerations in choreographing a good journey. The ultimate test of your prowess as a designer is to turn a group of young children loose on your path, and see what they do: If they skip, run, jump, or play hopscotch across it, then you've created a fine path indeed!

You can create mysterious meanders in huge forested regions or in the tiniest of courtyard spaces. You can place your plantings so they reveal or obscure views within a garden. The simple gesture of setting evergreen shrubs in the middle of your line of sight to the front door is an example. Now your destination point is hidden, and your formerly straight path of necessity curves around the plantings, carving out space, lengthening the journey, and creating a sense of mystery that hadn't existed there before. Creating surprises along the way is one of the delights of the path designer. The same evergreens, placed to block a distant view of a mountain, makes the vista far more powerful when it is finally revealed.

You can also bring mystery into your garden by choreographing the visitor's experience of light and shadow. When you follow a path that leads through the dappled light of a shady grove of pine trees into a sun-baked expanse of lawn and into a moist and mossy rhododendron dell, you delight in the complete and sudden contrast between spaces. Contracting and expanding; darkening and lightening; concealing and revealing; ascending and descending—playing with oppositions in your garden enhances and evokes the magic of your land. As designer, you become an illusionist: a magician whose sleight of hand delights, mystifies, and enchants all who enter.

THE MIND JOURNEY

When you arrive at the destination point of your physical journey, you stand at the departure point of your mind journey. What is a mind journey? Imagine the following scene: You are sitting in a wing chair in front of a hearth and gazing at a roaring fire. The high back and enclosing arms of the wing chair act as a secure viewing position from which you can contemplate freely; the hearth acts as a frame that sets the fire apart as special from the rest of the room; and the dancing flames are the focus of your attention—their ever-changing patterns create a dynamic point of visual attraction and mental concentration and an oasis of warmth for body and soul. Put together, these three elements offer a fascinating journey for the mind. You enjoy the same experience on an ocean beach when you lie against a dune and watch the waves breaking on the sand. Their rhythmic, ever-changing yet continuous patterns simultaneously lure your attention yet lull you into a dream state, calming you into a condition of near perfect peace. If you create a strong sense of security, of definition, and of visual interest in your garden, you will bring such a contemplative mind journey into your everyday life.

Viewing Position

A viewing position is a place where you stop to rest—the destination point of your physical journey and the departure point of your mind journey. Your viewing position may be any of the archetypal vantages:

the top of a hill, the edge of a stream, the inside of a cavelike grotto. It may be as simple as a flat-topped rock or as elaborate as a vine-clad pergola. What you need is simply a good vantage and a strong sense of protection that gives you a secure perch for contemplating your garden. Garden huts and backed-up benches are two good positions for viewing up, out, down on, or into your magic land.

Frame

A frame provides definition—either on the vertical or horizontal plane—for delineating the contemplative focal point. Imagine yourself standing on a mountain peak. You are above the tree line and all the other hills around you. You begin to view the world below, turning to look north, then east, then south, then west, then north again, and so on. You can't seem to stop yourself from pivoting in order to see the next view. Now imagine that cairns piled high with rocks were set so that they defined the view looking due north, east, south, and west. These vertical frames allow you to stop and contemplate the view to the north, segmenting it from the others as special. When you are tired of that view, you might turn to the eastern hills for a time. The act of framing delineates space and turns it into a landscape painting that you can study before moving your gaze or your body on to the next picturesque vista.

Many elements can be used for framing vistas. Tree trunks, fastigiate trees, and conical or topiaried shrubs can act as frames. Porch columns, French doors, mullioned windows, porticoes, and statuary are all architectural elements that are useful frames. Trellises, arbors, and grottoes can all be frames. The windows of garden-facing rooms in your house are frames. Often, the best frames are ones that you come on by surprise, such as a birch that becomes bent by the weight of snow along a woodsy lane. Those delineated views that you already know and love are also delightful as you anticipate seeing through them again. Without frames, you can't bring your mind into focus; and without a focus, you have no reason to contemplate.

Focus

The focus of the garden can be a single magnificent fountain or an extensive perennial border; a grand urban vista or a series of small woodland scenes along a path. In its archaic Latin meaning, the word *focus* refers to a fireplace or hearth—the central point of a home during the winter months. In a garden, the focus is the center of activity, the attraction drawing the greatest attention and interest, and the point of concentration or of expansion.

How do you create a focus for your garden? Perhaps your land already has a special "exclamation point" for you to work with, such as a natural stone outcropping, an old spring house, a view of a neighboring pond, or a stand of bamboo. Any of these objects can, with ingenuity, be turned into the point of focus for your garden. But more often than not, you won't have any natural amenities to work with. Instead, you will need to create a focus that is completely new to your land.

Ingenuity and imagination are required to create something from nothing, but an even more important requirement is a feeling of confidence. The next chapter offers a stimulating exercise that is guaranteed to teach you that you have what it takes to design your own garden. And it introduces you to some design principles that will prove useful as you create your magic land.

Chapter 11

Dynamic Balance

*Move the elements of your garden around
until you get them to feel just right.*

OST people I know are afraid to make aesthetic decisions in the garden. It seems strange to me, since they have no problem in making a "conversation area" in their living rooms or in arranging family photographs on a living room table. But at the same time they are fearful of placing a tree, a bench, a birdbath, or a flowerpot outside the backdoor. The following simple exercise shows you how much you already know about placing objects in space.

EXERCISE: MAKING A TABLETOP GARDEN

One night at the dinner table, before clearing all the dishes, start to arrange the plates, glasses, utensils, saltshakers, flower arrangement, and condiments so they "look right." First, choose a viewing position such as the head of the table, and sit there. Now imagine the saltshakers as statues, the glasses as trees, the table place mats as terraces, and the napkins as water. The utensils might represent a path (with a "fork" in the road!) and the leftovers might be rocks or plantings. Then ask family or friends to start arranging the items on the table so they feel balanced aesthetically and visually. Some will automatically choose a symmetrical composition, where the location of objects on the left match those on the right. But if one person simply moves the central plate off to one side, the symmetry is broken and everyone's innate aesthetic sense will be called into play in order to compose the "garden."

Ask each participant to take turns sitting at the viewing position and make any changes that they feel are necessary. You'll be amazed at the quickness of the decisions and agreement between parties about what feels right. You have designed a garden right there in the space of a few minutes, on top of your dining room table! Read through the next sections and notice how the principles of aesthetic decision making that I discuss apply to what you have created.

Dynamic Balance

· · · · · ·

You have designed a garden right there in the space of a few minutes, on top of your dining room table!

I have done this exercise with students using the leftovers from bag lunches or the contents of their briefcases and purses. In small seminars, I have asked students to design a whole room as a garden, using anything that is available in the classroom: coats, slide projectors, newsprint, tables, wastebaskets, and even the students themselves. I have cut up cardboard into different shapes and have had designers lay these out as a garden. I've sat in diners, cafés, and even the finest restaurants and have gotten my hosts or guests involved in arranging the available glassware so it looks perfect, only to have the waiter join in, adding a tie, a packet of sugar, or moving a plate a quarter of an inch to the left. I watch as my subjects realize that they are really adept at aesthetic decision making, and we all laugh uproariously as certain silly but appropriate decisions are made. Give this exercise a try—at a family meal, a dinner party, or in your garden.

Although we may not always realize it, we all get obsessive about arranging things: knickknacks on a display shelf; guest seating at a dinner party; pictures on a wall. The reason for this obsessive behavior is that we care about making things feel just right. You might plump the pillows before visitors arrive; you move each wine glass a half centimeter to the right; you straighten the rug so it lines up with the wall or arrange the flowers so the colors, heights, and textures appear harmonious. You know somehow when they feel right. The same thing that you understand about arranging items in your house also applies to composing the elements of your garden.

Every garden needs to be composed with a sense of "dynamic balance." This seems to be a paradoxical idea because if something is in balance, how can it be dynamic at the same time? Isn't something that is in balance most often static in its effect? Think about the difference between an equilateral, an isosceles, and a scalene triangle. The equilateral triangle is in a state of perfect balance: Each side is equal to the others. The isosceles triangle with its equal angles resting at the base and its unequal angle pointing to the sky, is also balanced, with one side symmetrical to the other. The scalene triangle, however, with each side being unequal to every other side, possesses a feeling of dynamic balance: dynamic by virtue of its asymmetry, yet balanced because it is a triangle, an inherently stable geometric form. Unless you are seeking to create a formal garden in which objects are placed symmetrically, you will find it useful to use the principle of dynamic balance as you place your trees, shrubs, flowers, stones, and sculptures in your garden. Following are some basic principles of object setting that I find useful in creating dynamic focal points for my gardens.

MOVEMENT IN A GARDEN

You can't focus on an object for long unless it feels as if it is in motion. Movement can be constant such as a recirculating stream or spray jet; or intermittent, such as a wind chime, a mobile, or a deer-scarer (a hollowed-out bamboo pipe that fills with water and creates a rhythmic clopping noise as it empties against a stone). Movement doesn't have to be actual; it can be something felt rather than seen: the raking patterns of Japanese stone gardens outline wave patterns as on a sea, but nothing in these gardens moves at all. Similarly, the best sculpture often gives the sense of movement where it doesn't actually exist.

Yet paradoxically, too much movement can be aesthetically jarring and visually chaotic to the viewer. Think of a three-ring circus going on in front of your eyes. Which ring do you look at first: the trapeze artist in ring one, the elephants in ring two; or the clowns in ring three? You can't concentrate on one thing if there is too much visual richness in your field of vision. Yet too little movement can be deadly dull. Think of the outdoor urban plazas that are found in so many of today's cities: a modern sculpture, often of Cortan steel, sits huge and motionless flanked by a phalanx of benches and a few spindly trees.

Movement is created by using four possible design techniques: lines of force, points of balance, repeating forms, and layering. In the next section, we take a closer look at these techniques and how they can animate your garden designs.

Lines of Force

All gardens — static or dynamic — are composed of three characteristic lines of force: the horizontal, the vertical, and the diagonal. Each bears a distinctive imprint on the personality of a garden. You may choose to base the design of your garden on one of these possibilities, or combine them as an aesthetically thrilling tour de force.

Gardens built around horizontal lines of force tend to be restful, calm, peaceful places. Think of a Zen garden, with its rectangular sandy sea on which mossy islands float: Its predominant line of force is horizontal. A horizontal line feels like a sunset on the horizon — low, lingering, long, and lean across a late afternoon landscape. The horizontal focal point lies across your picture plane and rests your eyes awhile on the land. A long sinewy stone wall that starts and ends low and acts as a parapet in between is a horizontal focal point; a lying stone, a swimming pool, and a raised perennial bed all emphasize the horizontal while carving out space. A quiet kind of focus, one that your eye skims across before coming back to pause there, the horizontal line is restful — a bed on which to sleep.

Not so the vertical line of force. Think of all your favorite monuments: the Washington Monument, the Eiffel Tower, the Statue of Liberty — essentially vertical lines in space that shout: "Look at me!" and we do. The vertical object demands our immediate and devoted attention because it stands out against the horizon line, rather than blending in; up against the contours of Mother Earth rather than nestling down beside her. When you gather a crowd of verticals together, you get a nest of egos, each demanding to be bigger than all the others. In a garden, think of a stand of sunflowers, a spate of bluebird houses, the sets of statues or topiary trees that anchor the axial paths at a formal garden like Versailles. To use verticals in the landscape is to garner attention—so use them well!

A diagonal line of force is always dramatic and never at rest. Seen in bird's-eye view, a diagonal knifes its way across a site, jagged or straight; it severs a square site into two equilateral triangles and seem to make it feel longer and bigger than it really is. Seen in elevation, straight on, a diagonal seems unfinished or out of balance unless another object is either supporting it at its base or offsetting its directionality by giving it a sense of completion. Think of the Leaning Tower of Pisa as it stands against its vertical and horizontal neighbors, or a carefully pruned pine that needs a crutch to hold up its heavy head across a pool, or a rock that gestures toward another in a grouping nearby. The implied movement of a diagonal line is intense and demands to be noticed—we follow a diagonal wherever it goes.

Points of Balance

A single object, which I call a *point*, whether placed on the horizontal, the vertical, or the diagonal, is often the focus of our gardens. Sometimes we want to feature a cosmic tree, an obelisk, a rose arch, or a pergola as the major point of interest around which the garden revolves. And revolve is exactly what happens with a singular object as focal point: The rest of the garden seems to circle around it, endlessly. It feels in perfect balance. In The New England Spring Flower Show, for example, we constructed a twelve-foot-high wrought-iron column as a stand for attaching five fifteen-foot-long nasturtium vines—creating a floral Maypole in the center of a rectangular space. The constraints of the layout and the central focus made all other decision making easy: ground cover and middle-story plantings were set out symmetrically in curvy, rhythmic lines.

The Magic Land
• • • • • •

Every object that you place in your garden possesses an *aura:* defined by Webster's dictionary as a "distinctive atmosphere surrounding a given source; a luminous radiation." Although I am not able to prove this scientifically, I believe that each object, animate or inanimate, carries with it its own area of influence or atmosphere that we need to account for as we design our gardens. Sometimes there are practical reasons for an aura: You need to leave breathing room around a tree for it to grow or allow a statue to enjoy an appropriate amount of open space around it for it to be seen in the round. But sometimes an object won't feel right unless you express its aura in the landscape. In a Japanese dry landscape garden, for example, gravel is used to represent water. Any object, such as a solitary stone or an island grouping that interrupts the lines of the gravel "sea," possesses an aura—a raked line of gravel that encircles the object, suggesting the wave patterns that would form naturally around it.

Let me explain how including an aura around an object can help you make design decisions. Some years ago we created a new deck for the owner of a Victorian house. The client was a weekend sailor, so we decided to design a deck that felt like the prow of a ship. The new three-tiered structure protruded on an angle into the surrounding lawn, which felt like a verdant sea of grass when you sat on the deck. The strength of its boatlike form and the feeling of movement that it produced seemed to need a strong edge to "stop" it from moving into the neighbor's yard. So we built a tiered stone sitting wall with angles that echoed the lines of the deck—a "berth" at the edge of the "mainland" where you could watch the "ship" as it seemed to sail toward you. The wall was the deck's aura displaced to the edge of the property. Without it, the project would not have felt complete.

If you choose to work with two points as focal objects, one way is to use them as mirror images of each other. For instance, you could place two identical fish pools to balance each other symmetrically on either side of a path. Another way is to use them to create an artificial sense of relative distance. For example, if you place a tall object in the foreground and a short object in the background, you create a greater sense of depth than if the two had been the same height. Similarly, if the front object is short and the back one tall, you pull the background right into the foreground, collapsing space rather than enlarging it. Whatever you do, make sure that you do not line up two similar objects on the same axis as your main viewing position. The one in back will disappear behind the foreground object, creating an odd sense of imbalance and imprecision to the design, as though you didn't care enough about the object to show it off. Always check your design to make sure that the points—the plants, rocks, statues, or other focal points—don't line up.

INTIMATE IMMENSITY

When you were a child, weren't you fascinated by things that were tiny and by things that were huge? Anthills and their minute residents; elephants and their engorged bodies; miniature dollhouses and sprawling castles; intricate snowdomes and gargantuan glaciers. Anything that wasn't one's own size offered powerful possibilities for the imagination.

The same holds true in our adult life—intimate and immense things continue to delight. Part of the enchantment lies in a paradox: When I look at something that is tiny, like a snowdome, am I immense or intimate in relation to it? Obviously, my body is huge, yet I can shrink myself to "inhabit" the space in my mind, so I must also be tiny. When I look at the presidential faces on Mount Rushmore, am I tiny or huge in relation to them? Again, my body is tiny, but my mind is huge as it rushes to examine Roosevelt's face close-up.

This paradox can be applied to garden design as well. We delight in miniature landscapes: bonsai trees, terrariums, model train gardens, rockeries, heather gardens, little urban courtyards, tray gardens: dwarfed versions of everyday reality that fascinate because of their smallness. Oversize garden objects also draw us: ancient beech forests, the massive sculpture set in art parks, mammoth rock outcroppings, distant mountain vistas made part of the garden scene.

Three or more points are a challenge and a pleasure to work with in a design. In a recent flower show design we used a handsome wooden outdoor garden chair that sat on an angle looking out at the visitors (who in turn looked in at it) as our main focal point. Behind it, we placed a weeping jasmine tree, in full yellow flower, which draped its lovely branches over the chair, to create a kind of bower. To either side of the chair, we set tall calla lilies, to anchor the triangular shape of the backdrop. This created a placid and balanced effect, but it seemed flat and unfinished — not very mysterious. The addition of two abutilon trees — flowering maples — placed asymmetrically in the front and sides of the exhibit closed in the view by framing it, yet acted like two points that brought to life the main focal point, the jasmine tree with the chair under it. Playing with three points to create a sense of asymmetric balance endows a design with a sense of movement and dynamism.

In a symmetrical world, two objects must be in perfect balance to uphold the pattern; in an asymmetrical world, three or more

When I look at something that is tiny, like a snowdome, am I immense or intimate in relation to it?

objects can create a sense of balance through triangulation—placing them so they form a nonequilateral triangle in space. The result is that the garden feels dynamic, because its focal points are irregularly placed, yet balanced if they have a clear relationship one to another.

Repeating Forms

I once took the train to Ise, home of the most sacred religious shrine in Japan. Standing near the station were two huge stone temple lanterns of the kasuga type typically placed in front of a shrine or temple compound. I caught a bus to the shrine itself, some five miles out of town. As we drove, I noticed more of these lanterns along the route. Near town, they could be found every few thousand feet. But the closer we got to the shrine, the closer together the lanterns seemed to stand until we reached the shrine itself, by which time they created an uninterrupted line of lanterns on either side of the road. The repetition and increasing intensity of these forms created a wonderful sense of anticipation and arrival on the processional journey that I made to the Ise Shrine.

Repeating forms is always a good principle to use in any design, whether geometric or natural. Repetition allows the viewer to unconsciously pick out and pay attention to the most important variables as different from the rest of an assemblage. Perhaps it is a color that repeats, such as burgundy red or silvery gray. It could be a shape, such as a weeping form, a lozenge, or a triangular shape. You can even repeat a certain texture, such as a mossy ground cover or a needleleaf spire. It could be a rhythmic pattern, like repeating S-curves of boxwood that form evergreen swoops in a planting bed. Or maybe you love birches and repeatedly use their vertical form and white bark to unite disparate parts of your garden. You may want a white-on-white pattern, where the birches emerge from white flowering hydrangeas. Repetition allows you to give a satisfying unity to the design of your landscape.

Another method in creating dynamic balance in your garden has to do with the relation between the foreground, the middleground, and the background. This is also attained by a repetition of forms. My brother's house in New Mexico sits high on a hill overlooking a ridge of rocky juniper-clad mountain peaks. When he enlarged his kitchen, he saw an opportunity to take full advantage of this dramatic setting by capturing the best view with a large greenhouse window over the sink, the focal point of his new room. In this window, a collection of gray-green dwarf cacti forms the foreground; outside, a set of tall windswept juniper trees frame a view of a perfectly triangulated mountain peak, forming the middleground, and the wide arm of the distant ridge forms the background, all linked by the similar texture and color of the vegetation. Had he chosen to place geraniums in the sunny window, the effect created by "borrowing the landscape" would have been spoiled. Such design decisions are subtle but important. By repeating forms in clearly demarcated planes of space, you can achieve a sense of dynamic balance in your garden.

Layers

While you are working on your garden plan, think in terms of *all* the techniques just described: lines of force, points of balance, and repeating forms; but it's important to experiment with layering the design on your land, perhaps the most useful design idea for creating harmony and movement in your garden. If you look back to your table garden, you'll see that the way you started to create it was by layering the forms, placing the flower arrangement first, then moving the plates around, then trying the cups in various locations, and finally getting the silverware to work on the groundplane. You do the same thing when you build your real garden. Let me explain.

To layer something is to place one thickness or fold over another: to create a buildup of different forms that, taken together, create a harmonious whole. You can layer on the vertical plane — in from a garden's enclosure, or on the horizontal plane — up from a garden's floor. Layering helps in design because you can make decisions sequentially, using all the principles described to create an aesthetically pleasing garden, in which materials, forms, textures, and colors all "work" because you have added them slowly and carefully, observing the effect of a potential new decision over time. For instance, if you wanted to create a perimeter screening of trees to block your property from view of your neighbor, then you might erect a fence, and layer conifer and deciduous trees in front of it, to give a woodsy, natural look. You might choose to step the enclosure down in heights, with tallest trees in the background, larger rhododendrons in the middleground, and smaller shrubs in the foreground. Or you might decide to work with points, placing the three tallest trees asymmetrically. You might choose to repeat forms; using the bright red stems of the red-twigged dogwood to play against the bloodgrass that you have planted in the foreground.

I layer my design when I start construction on a garden, amassing my materials in one place and building the garden in "courses." If it is a small rock garden that I am building, for example, I start with the enclosure course, first installing any perimeter fences and interior walls. Then I move to the grading course to create the hills and valleys and ponds or stream beds that are part of the design. Next I work on the rock course, making sure that I have all the large and small stones stockpiled close by so I can place them as I need them — usually during an intense and often dangerous day requiring quick and sure decision making. Then I amass all my major plant materials into one place, including trees and the larger shrubs, and place them in relation to the stones. Finally, I complete the planting course by installing small shrubs and perennials, ground covers, and bulbs on the floor of the garden. In this way, I layer my design, making one design decision after another that works aesthetically with the design decisions before it. Each course should work on its own; each additional course should enrich and enliven the course before it. My purpose is always to make a dynamic yet balanced design by placing these myriad objects in layers so they feel just right — not boring and never predictable.

Layering offers the designer the possibility of growth and change as you continue to add to, subtract from, and therefore improve the garden over the years that you own it. It's like tinkering—you tinker all the time to make something right. I like to think that you are adding layers of magic to it over the years and that each addition fits into its place with a feeling of inevitability.

Great gardeners are always tinkering. They can't keep their hands off their land. They keep trying to express their garden's magic in new ways, better ways, better colors, longer blooms—and as the garden grows, new unimagined things continue to happen to it. Hedges fill out, shrubs overgrow their bed, perennials multiply profusely or get choked out by other more vigorous plants. New objects get added and new garden areas are created to set them off. Old gardens get pulled out to make room for yet another new idea. Great gardeners seem to endow their gardens with the gift of continuous newness.

Chapter 12

Hearing the Stream with Open Eyes

The ideas in one art form apply to all art forms.

FEW years ago I found this line from an ancient Japanese haiku poem by Shutaku: "Hearing the stream with open eyes." I immediately felt that it perfectly expressed the paradox and pleasures of garden design, because to become a great designer in any art form one must always be in a state of "hearing the stream with *open eyes*"—facing the world with childlike openness, seeing a situation freshly, as for the first time, again and again. Further, in *hearing* the stream, we open our heart to the design problem at hand and let it and not our intellect speak the solution. We *hear* with our *eyes* when we "design freely" as my garden master used to advise— not abiding by any rules or conventions, but creating every design as a response to the site and its conditions, to the plants we hope to

A great designer must always be in a state of "hearing the stream with open eyes"—facing the world with childlike openness.

use, and to the forms that we want to express on our land. As such, each garden should be something that has never been seen before.

When we hear a *stream*, we realize that we exist as a part of a continuum, including the natural processes of nature, of history, and of knowledge. By knowing our place in the stream, we become humble and seek always to tread with care and respect and to continue to learn as both we and our gardens grow. By seeking creative collaborations with others, we become part of a stream of knowledge, because working with contractors, engineers, geologists, hydrologists, horticulturists, and historians can expand our information base and offer us new ways of seeing what we think we already know. The image of a stream also suggests what we all delight and despair in as we work in our gardens and in our lives: that there is a process of continuity and change—a course that continues flowing even as the channel changes its shape, its depth, its direction.

Finally, "hearing the stream with open eyes" suggests a mixed metaphor: Using one sense to understand another. Recently, I employed all my senses and sensibilities to design a "music garden" with cellist Yo-Yo Ma to be built in a metropolitan park in Toronto. He wanted the design to be based on a piece of music: the First Suite for Unaccompanied Cello by Johann Sebastian Bach. I decided to listen to the music "with open eyes" to understand the feelings and the images that it evoked in me. Based on ancient dance forms, the suite is divided into six movements: the prelude, the allemande, the courante, the sarabande, the minuet, and the gigue, each suggesting a different time signature, structure, and emotion that I could use to translate into form on the land.

As I listened with my eyes, the design began to evolve. The prelude became an undulating riverscape, the allemande a deep forest, the courante a whirling wildflower meadow, and the sarabande a perfectly round-hedged garden room. The minuet felt like a formal parterre garden and the gigue a lively and colorful set of steps that tumbled you back into the real world outside the high-hedged garden walls. Our vision: a creative collaboration between musician and designer to create a magic land for a public space, where music would always be playing and performance would abound. Wait and see, one day soon, a music garden may be part of every city, bringing people the harmonious beauties of music and garden, allowing them to truly "hear the stream with open eyes."

Index

Index

• • • • • •

Index

• • • • • •

Index
● ● ● ● ● ●